D062646I

CLIMBERS AND
WALL PLANTS

CLIMBERS AND
WALL PLANTS

ALAN TITCHMARSH

WARD LOCK LIMITED · LONDON

ACKNOWLEDGEMENTS

The publishers gratefully acknowledge the following agencies for granting permission to reproduce the colour photographs: the Harry Smith Horticultural Photographic Collection (pp. 2, 11, 15, 22, 27, 30, 43, 51, 59, 62, 71, 90 and 91); and Pat Brindley (pp. 35, 38, 42, 54, 67, 75 and 82). Cover picture courtesy of Pat Brindley: *Clematis* × *jackmanii* 'Superba'.

All the line drawings are by Nils Solberg.

© Ward Lock Limited 1987

First published in Great Britain in 1987
by Ward Lock Limited, 8 Clifford
Street, London W1X 1RB
An Egmont Company

All Rights Reserved. No part of this
publication may be reproduced, stored
in a retrieval system, or transmitted, in
any form or by any means, electronic,
mechanical, photocopying, recording,
or otherwise, without the prior
permission of the Copyright owners.

House editor Denis Ingram

Text filmset in Bembo by
Paul Hicks Limited
Middleton, Manchester

Printed in Portugal

British Library Cataloguing in Publication Data
Titchmarsh, Alan, *1949*
    Climbers and wall plants.–2nd Ed.
    1. Climbing plants
    I. Title
    635.9'6   SB427

    ISBN 0-7063-6509-7

Frontispiece: The soft, downy leaves of *Abutilon vitofolium* 'Album' are decorated with pure white 'tissue-paper' mallow flowers in summer.

CONTENTS

PREFACE

The country cottage, swathed in its cloak of creepers and clematis, never fails to draw sighs of admiration; but how many of its captivated admirers fight shy of using the plants on their own houses in the mistaken belief that all they will bring is a mixture of rising damp and spiders? As if this wasn't enough, the plants' roots are accused of lifting foundations, and their tendrils of dislodging mortar.

If all these accusations had some truth in them, country cottages would have long since bitten the dust. In reality, if the right plant is chosen for a particular situation, and if it is established and supported properly, you can look forward to years of trouble-free cultivation.

Walls are not the only places that give opportunity for growing this varied range of plants. Trellis-work and fencing, arches and arbours, pergolas and old trees can all be used as support systems for a large selection of flowering and foliage plants which have a tendency to travel upwards.

Rampant climbers make excellent screens for sheds and garden eyesores, but don't make the mistake of thinking that all climbers need masses of space; if you can lay your hands on a wooden tub and a tripod of bamboo canes the beauty of morning glories and the scent of sweet peas can be yours in just a few months – the time it takes to raise them from seeds.

To me, the greatest feature of all these adventurous plants is their ability to make the house a part of the garden by bringing their flowers right up to the windows; and when grown in the open on free-standing supports they can add height to an otherwise flat and shapeless display.

Almost any shrub can be planted against a wall, but for the purposes of this compact little book I have chosen plants which lend themselves to this kind of cultivation by virtue of their habit of growth, or because they are not completely hardy and so can be grown with a much greater degree of success in the sheltered environment a wall provides.

If this book can persuade you to grow just one climber or wall plant without worrying it has done its job.

Beech, Hampshire   A.T.

· CHAPTER 1 ·

SUITABLE SITES

You may have decided where you want to put your climber, but stop for a moment and consider how a plant climbs; it will help you to choose the right subject and support system for your situation.

Climbers originally learned to climb for a reason – to get at the light which enables them to produce food and therefore survive – and they developed several different techniques; some plants, such as honeysuckle, go clockwise, others, such as convolvulus, go anticlockwise but whichever direction taken, twiners need some kind of framework to wrap themselves around.

Other plants have gone one stage further and developed twining leaf stalks, and among the most efficient climbers from our point of view are those which have developed tendrils – little snake-like outgrowths which spread out like feelers and clasp anything likely to provide support. The tendrils on many plants are equipped with adhesive pads allowing adhesion to both smooth and rough surfaces.

The aerial roots on ivy are tenacious enough to do almost as well as

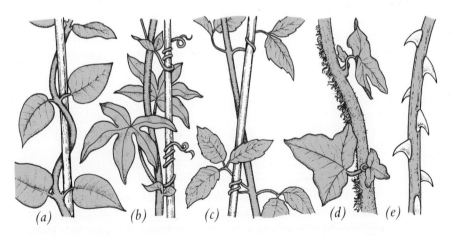

Fig. 1 Climbing plants have developed several different techniques of reaching the top of trees and other handy supports: (a) twining stems (b) tendrils; (c) twining leaf stalks; (d) aerial roots; (e) thorns

adhesive tendrils, but they do need a surface which is slightly rough if they are to get a good grip.

Rambling and climbing roses get a certain amount of help from their thorns, but these are seldom stout enough to support the plants completely and additional restraint is nearly always necessary if the plants are to be kept in good shape.

WALLS

In the garden, or even on a balcony or patio, you can nearly always find a wall that would be brightened up by the leaves and flowers of a wall shrub or climber.

However, there are several important points to bear in mind before planting. I mentioned earlier that people often worry needlessly about the adverse effects that climbing plants have on house walls. You do not need to worry about the foundations of the house; most of the plants recommended in this book do not have root systems of a sufficient size to cause any problems – real damage is done only when vigorous trees are planted in clay soils which are excessively wet in winter and which dry out and crack in summer. What you should avoid doing is planting a climber which clings by aerial roots or adhesive tendrils directly against the wall if your house is covered with pebbledash. The eventual weight of the plant may peel the cement off the wall in a large sheet. This is not to say you cannot grow plants with such climbing adaptations if you own a pebbledashed house; the answer is to equip the walls with some kind of wire or trellis framework which can take their weight.

On well-mortared brick or stone walls, self-clinging plants should cause no problems if they are pruned or clipped each year so that their

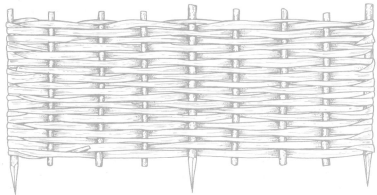

Fig. 2 Wattle hurdle

weight is reduced. Those which twine or are equipped with twining tendrils should again be provided with a wire or a trellis framework which is firmly attached a few inches from the wall's surface. (More detail on these supports is given in Chapter 6.) Choose plants for your walls carefully: take into account their eventual height and plant only those which you can keep in shape without too much effort. Very vigorous Virginia creepers are fine for covering a house wall but you must be prepared to trim the shoots around windows and gutters. There are other climbers which involve much less work.

FENCES AND SCREENS

There is a vast range of fencing and screening material available today, and much of it can support plant growth without the aid of any additional framework. Hazel and wattle hurdles are rustic and fairly long lasting; chestnut palings are more open if a solid barrier is undesirable, and large panels of trellis-work are pleasing to look at whether clad in foliage or not. That ubiquitous interwoven fencing has a smart appearance but it does offer a lot of wind resistance and will frequently blow down in strong gusts. If you want to grow anything but ivy and Virginia creeper up it you will have to nail on some horizontal wires.

One word on creosote. If plant foliage gets near wood recently treated with this tar-derived preservative it will be badly burned. Use instead copper naphthenate which is available as Cuprinol. Once dry this does not affect plants at all.

If you have chain-link fencing, don't despair. It may look bare and uninteresting, but it offers excellent support to a whole host of climbers whether they twine, cling or scramble. The plastic-covered kind is best because the galvanized type can shed quantities of zinc when it is rained on, until eventually a toxicity builds up in the soil.

ARCHES AND PERGOLAS

A rustic arch over which honeysuckle or roses are trained makes a delightful entrance to any garden. Larch poles treated with a wood preservative are obtainable quite cheaply from any good garden centre or nursery and you do not need a degree in woodwork to knock together a fairly stable archway (Fig. 3a). For the more ambitious with a longer pathway, a series of arches can be joined together to form a pergola, and a different climbing plant trained up each column (Fig. 3b).

A pergola may be as simple or as elaborate as you care to make it.

The columns can be made of wood, brick or stone, and the horizontal supports of rustic or prepared timber. Galvanized staples can be knocked into the wooden supports, and through them garden twine can be passed to hold in wayward stems.

TRIPODS AND COLONNADES

If you do not have room for something as grand as a pergola, a tripod of rustic poles would be a suitable compromise. Only a square metre or so of ground is needed, where three poles can be inserted and tied at the top as shown in Fig.3c. All manner of climbers will be happy to grow up this support (though they will need tying in), and it can add height to an otherwise flat garden. Smaller versions made with stout bamboo canes can be used as supports for annual climbers that will be resident in the garden through just one summer.

Fig. 3 (a) Arch; (b) pergola; (c) tripod; (d) colonnade

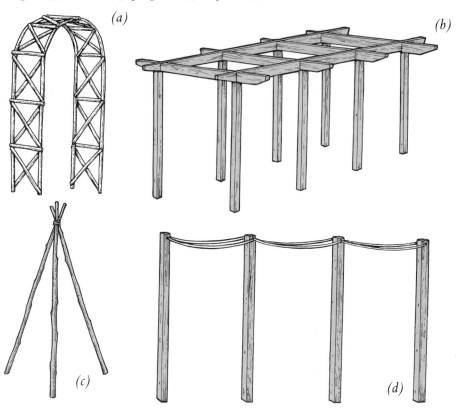

(a) *(b)* *(c)* *(d)*

Boldness of leaf and a talent for turning bright scarlet in autumn have assured the elephantine *Vitis coignetiae* of a secure future in British gardens.

Colonnades are seldom seen today except in the gardens of stately homes. They usually consist of a series of tall, sturdy wooden posts which stand in a long line and are linked by one or two thick ropes (Fig. 3d). Climbing and rambling roses look good when grown on colonnades, but they have to be attended to fairly regularly if they are to be kept within the confines of the support system.

TREES

Old fruit trees that are well past their prime, and other trees that appear dull and uninteresting, can make excellent climbing frames for clematis, roses and other rampant growers. Even if the tree is dead it can be left to accommodate these scrambling guests who will spill their blooms from its branches through the summer and, in the case of some clematis, decorate them with fluffy seedheads in winter.

Plant the climber two feet from the tree and provide it with good soil and a cane to bring it into contact with the trunk.

Tree stumps a couple of metres high can be used to support rambling roses and scrambling plants such as celastrus and ivy; so if the job of removing the hefty stump of a felled tree fills you with horror, drop the idea and plant a climber at the foot of it. Soon it will be transformed into a column of foliage and flowers.

BUILDINGS

Ugly garden sheds and other eyesores can easily be masked (and often taken over) by a vigorous-growing climber. Provide some wire or trellis supports if the walls are smooth, or choose a plant that will cling on its own. You will have to trim the growth back drastically every few months if you choose a very vigorous plant, and the stems may well force their way inside. Take your pick: either be patient and plant something slow growing which will take less time to maintain, or plant a polygonum (Russian vine) and stand by with the shears.

CONTAINERS

For the gardener who is really short of space, tubs and large pots provide a means of growing a much wider range of plants.

Only good-sized containers should be planted up with climbers, for the plants do need room to spread their roots. A tripod of bamboo canes may be inserted to support annual climbers, or the container may be set at the foot of a wall fitted with wires or trellis if more vigorous plants are used (Fig. 5).

Fig. 4 Old fruit trees make excellent climbing frames for clematis, roses and other rampant growers

Fig. 5 Climber on cane tripod in tub

CHAPTER 2

A PLANT FOR EVERY SITUATION

Don't despair because your wall faces north, or because your soil is a heavy clay, for there are at least a handful of plants that will enjoy these seemingly unpleasant conditions.

The following lists will help you to choose the right plants for your garden, but don't be afraid to experiment a little as well. If the plant you want to grow does not appear in the list appropriate to your situation it may well be unsuited to it. If this fills you with disappointment, take a risk and give the plant a try; it may well succeed, for no two gardens have exactly the same soil or climate, and a plant that refuses to grow in your neighbour's garden may thrive in yours.

Botanical names are used here to make it easier for you to locate the plants in the A – Z section, but if these mouthfuls strike terror into your heart, common names are included in the index at the back of the book to enable you to trace the plant you know so well by an English name.

PLANTS FOR NORTH-FACING WALLS

Camellia species and varieties
Celastrus orbiculatus
Chaenomeles species and varieties
Choisya ternata
Clematis species and varieties
Cotoneaster horizontalis
Cotoneaster microphyllus
Escallonia macrantha
Forsythia suspensa and varieties
Garrya elliptica
Hedera species and varieties
Hydrangea petiolaris
Jasminum nudiflorum
Kerria japonica 'Pleniflora'
Parthenocissus species
Piptanthus laburnifolius
Schizophragma species
Tropaeolum speciosum

PLANTS FOR SOUTH-FACING WALLS

Abutilon species
Actinidia kolomikta
Ampelopsis species
Callistemon species
Campsis species
Carpenteria californica
Ceanothus species and varieties
Chaenomeles species and varieties
Chimonanthus praecox
Choisya ternata

Clianthus puniceus
Cobaea scandens
Convolvulus cneorum
Coronilla species
Cytisus battandieri
Eccremocarpus scaber
Escallonia species and varieties
Forsythia suspensa and varieties
Fremontodendron californicum
Humulus species and varieties
Ipomoea varieties
Itea ilicifolia

Lippia citriodora
Lonicera species and varieties
Magnolia grandiflora
Parthenocissus species
Passiflora caerulea
Phygelius capensis
Pyracantha species and varieties
Roses (climbers and ramblers)
Senecio species
Solanum species
Vitis coignetiae
Wisteria species

PLANTS FOR EAST-FACING WALLS

Celastrus orbiculatus
Chaenomeles species and varieties
Clematis species and varieties
Cotoneaster horizontalis
Cotoneaster microphyllus
Escallonia macrantha
Forsythia suspensa and varieties
Garrya elliptica

Hedera species and varieties
Hydrangea petiolaris
Jasminum nudiflorum
Kerria japonica 'Pleniflora'
Lonicera species and varieties
Parthenocissus species
Pyracantha species and varieties
Tropaeolum speciosum

PLANTS FOR WEST-FACING WALLS

Abutilon vitifolium
Actinidia kolomikta
Callistemon species
Camellia species and varieties
Carpenteria californica
Ceanothus species and varieties
Chaenomeles species and varieties
Chimonanthus praecox
Clematis species and varieties
Cobaea scandens
Cytisus battandieri
Escallonia species and varieties

Forsythia suspensa and varieties
Fremontodendron californicum
Garrya elliptica
Hedera species and varieties
Humulus species and varieties
Ipomoea varieties
Jasminum nudiflorum
Lonicera species and varieties
Magnolia grandiflora
Passiflora caerulea
Roses (climbers and ramblers)
Solanum crispum
Wisteria species

PLANTS FOR COASTAL GARDENS

Abutilon species*
Camellia species and varieties*
Carpenteria californica*

Ceanothus species*
Choisya ternata*
Clematis species and varieties*

*Clianthus puniceus**
*Convolvulus cneorum**
Coronilla species*
Cotoneaster species
*Cytisus battandieri**
*Eccremocarpus scaber**
Escallonia species and varieties*
*Fremontodendron californicum**
Garrya elliptica

Hydrangea petiolaris
*Lippia citriodora**
*Passiflora caerulea**
*Phygelius capensis**
Polygonum baldschuanicum
Pyracantha species and varieties
Senecio species*
Solanum species*

* These need the protection afforded by a south- or west-facing wall if they are to do well.

PLANTS FOR HEAVY CLAY SOILS

Abutilon vitifolium
Actinidia species
Camellia species and varieties
Celastrus species
Chaenomeles species and varieties
Choisya ternata
Clematis species and varieties
Cobaea scandens
Cotoneaster species
Cytisus battandieri
Escallonia species and varieties
Forsythia suspensa and varieties

Garrya elliptica
Hedera species and varieties
Jasminum nudiflorum
Kerria japonica 'Pleniflora'
Laburnum species
Magnolia grandiflora
Parthenocissus species
Piptanthus laburnifolius
Polygonum baldschuanicum
Roses (climbers and ramblers)
Senecio species
Wisteria species

If I had to pick the best garden camelia this would be it: the variety of *Camellia* × *williamsii* called 'Donation'.

PLANTS FOR LIGHT SANDY SOILS

Abutilon species
Actinidia species
Campsis species
Ceanothus species and varieties
Chaenomeles species and
 varieties
Choisya ternata
Clianthus puniceus
Cotoneaster species
Cytisus battandieri
Eccremocarpus scaber
Escallonia species and varieties
Forsythia suspensa and varieties
Fremontodendron californicum
Garrya elliptica

Hedera species and varieties
Jasminum species
Kerria japonica 'Pleniflora'
Laburnum species
Lippia citriodora
Lonicera species and varieties
Magnolia grandiflora
Parthenocissus species
Passiflora caerulea
Piptanthus laburnifolius
Polygonum baldschuanicum
Roses (climbers and ramblers)
Senecio species
Solanum species
Wisteria species

PLANTS FOR CHALKY SOILS

Abutilon species
Ceanothus species
Chaenomeles species and varieties
Chimonanthus praecox
Choisya ternata
Clematis species and varieties
Convolvulus cneorum
Coronilla species
Cotoneaster species
Cytisus battandieri
Escallonia species and varieties
Forsythia suspensa and varieties
Fremontodendron californicum

Garrya elliptica
Hedera species and varieties
Jasminum nudiflorum
Kerria japonica 'Pleniflora'
Laburnum species and varieties
Lippia citriodora
Lonicera species and varieties
Magnolia grandiflora
Polygonum baldschuanicum
Pyracantha species and varieties
Roses (climbers and ramblers)
Senecio species
Wisteria species

PLANTS FOR ACID SOILS

Abutilon species
Actinidia species
Camellia species and varieties
Campsis species
Chaenomeles species and varieties
Clianthus puniceus
Cobaea scandens
Cotoneaster species
Cucurbita species

Forsythia suspensa and varieties
Garrya elliptica
Hedera species and varieties
Jasminum species
Kerria japonica 'Pleniflora'
Laburnum species
Lippia citriodora
Lonicera species and varieties
Magnolia grandiflora

Parthenocissus species
Passiflora caerulea
Piptanthus laburnifolius
Polygonum baldschuanicum

Roses (climbers and ramblers)
Senecio species
Solanum species
Wisteria species

PLANTS WITH ORNAMENTAL FLOWERS

Abutilon species
Callistemon species
Camellia species and varieties
Campsis species
Carpenteria californica
Ceanothus species and varieties
Chaenomeles species and varieties
Chimonanthus praecox
Choisya ternata
Clematis species and varieties
Clianthus puniceus
Cobaea scandens
Convolvulus cneorum
Coronilla species
Cytisus battandieri
Eccremocarpus scaber
Escallonia species and varieties
Forsythia suspensa and varieties
Fremontodendron californicum
Garrya elliptica

Hydrangea petiolaris
Ipomoea varieties
Itea ilicifolia
Jasminum species
Kerria japonica 'Pleniflora'
Laburnum species
Lathyrus species and varieties
Lonicera species and varieties
Magnolia grandiflora
Passiflora species
Phygelius species
Piptanthus laburnifolius
Polygonum baldschuanicum
Roses (climbers and ramblers)
Schizophragma species
Senecio species
Solanum species
Thunbergia alata
Tropaeolum species and varieties
Wisteria species

PLANTS WITH ORNAMENTAL FOLIAGE

Actinidia kolomikta
Ampelopsis species
Choisya ternata
Convolvulus cneorum
Hedera species and varieties
Humulus species and varieties

Lippia citriodora
Lonicera japonica aureoreticulata
Magnolia grandiflora
Parthenocissus species
Senecio species
Vitis species

PLANTS WITH ORNAMENTAL FRUITS

Actinidia chinensis
Ampelopsis brevipedunculata
Celastrus species
Chaenomeles species and varieties
Cotoneaster species
Cucurbita species

Humulus species and varieties
Lonicera periclymenum and
   varieties
Passiflora caerulea
Pyracantha species and varieties
Vitis species

CHAPTER 3

A-Z OF CLIMBERS AND WALL PLANTS

ABUTILON

There are two species of abutilon which are well worth cultivating outdoors in sheltered gardens if they can be given the protection of a warm wall. In colder counties they will not survive the winter. *Abutilon megapotamicum* is perhaps the more tender and certainly the more compact grower of the two and will reach a height of between 1.25 and 2.5 m (4–8 ft). Its neat, dark green pointed leaves are carried on thin wiry stems from which drip dainty red and yellow bell-like blooms, each one tipped with a clapper of maroon stamens. The plant will bloom freely from summer to autumn and it has an attractive variety 'Variegatum' with yellow-mottled leaves.

The larger *A. vitifolium* is quite different in appearance. Its long and rather pithy stems carry large maple-shaped leaves coated in soft down, giving them a greyish hue. The pale lilac mallow-like blooms tone in perfectly with this muted colour scheme on a plant that may be anything from 3–9 m (10–30 ft) tall. *A. vitifolium* has a shorter flowering season than its more diminutive relation (between late spring and midsummer) but it makes up for its brevity by being quietly spectacular. On a warm wall at the Royal Horticultural Society's garden at Wisley, Surrey, it is planted so that the stems of *Solanum crispum* 'Glasnevin' run through its branches; the two flower at the same time and the effect is magical.

If the pale lilac of the straight species does not appeal to you (though the strength of tone does seem to vary) you can plump for the darker variety 'Veronica Tennant' or the white 'Album'.

POSITION AND SOIL

A sheltered south-facing wall is the best way of guaranteeing that these two rather tender deciduous plants survive, and a well-nourished and well-drained soil is greatly to their liking.

CULTIVATION

Plant in spring. Heavy applications of fertilizer and mulches of manure are not demanded, but *A. vitifolium* may drop its unopened flower buds if the soil is allowed to dry out in mid and late spring. It can also be a rather short-lived plant and may die inexplicably after several years of a seemingly happy existence. Do not let this put you off growing what is an otherwise excellent wall shrub.

PRUNING AND TRAINING

The main leading shoot of *A. vitifolium* should always be retained and tied in to trellis-work or wires held some distance from the wall by vine eyes or bolts. The largest lateral shoots can be carefully tied in as they grow to prevent them from being rocked and broken by wind. *A. megapotamicum* spreads more horizontally and only its longest stems need to be tied to trellis or wires.

With *A. vitifolium*, remove faded flower heads to prevent seed formation (unless seeds are needed for propagation) and prune out frost-damaged wood in spring. A little older wood can be removed from *A. megapotamicum* each spring.

PROPAGATION

A. vitifolium can be raised from seeds sown in gentle heat under glass in midwinter, or cuttings of firm young growths can be rooted in a propagating frame in summer. *A. megapotamicum* is best increased by rooting cuttings of firm young growths in a propagating frame in mid- to late summer.

ACTINIDIA

If you want a climbing plant guaranted to stop passers-by in their tracks, choose *Actinidia kolomikta*. Plant it against a warm wall and on many of the heart-shaped green leaves at least half the surface area will turn pink and white in summer. You will need a little patience with the plant – it may be rather dull for the first few years – but in a warm spot its leaves should colour up annually once it has settled in. I have heard that a little lime applied to the soil can encourage variegation in reluctant plants.

Most often *A. kolomikta* seems to grow only 2 or 2.5 m (6 or 8 ft) high, but it has been known to reach 6 m (20 ft). Pruning will enable your specimen to be kept to the height best suited to your needs.

The other species worth growing is *A. chinensis*, the Chinese gooseberry. This variety, like *A. kolomikta,* is deciduous but it has a faster rate of growth and its twining stems covered in red hairs will climb over old tree stumps, trees and buildings, displaying their heart-shaped leaves, cream to yellow flowers and hairy egg-shaped fruits. The plant may eventually reach 9 m (30 ft) and is valuable more for its masking effect than any special beauty. Its fruits are edible and you may consider them as a bonus – but make sure that the plant you buy has flowers with both male and female parts or you will end up fruitless, unless you plant both a known male and a female.

POSITION AND SOIL

Any ordinary soil, moderately enriched with compost or manure at planting time, suits actinidias, and apart from *A. kolomikta*, which colours best on a south- or west-facing wall, they will thrive in partial shade as well as in good light. Walls, old tree stumps and trees, pergolas, arches and buildings can all act as supports for these plants which climb by means of twining stems.

CULTIVATION

Plant in spring or autumn. Both shrubs are accommodating and vigorous enough to survive with very little encouragement.

PRUNING AND TRAINING

Because of their twining habit these shrubs do need something to cling to, be it wires, trellis or tree branches. Provide the support and they will do the rest. Keep a good framework of branches on the support system (if the plant is being grown on a wall) and shorten back unwanted growths to 15 cm (6 in) during the summer as soon as they are about a metre (yard) long. In winter cut the side growths back to two or three buds and tie in one or two new long stems, cutting out a few old ones. When the plants are trained through trees or over buildings it will be sufficient to thin them out in winter and cut off unwanted growths in summer.

PROPAGATION

Cuttings of firm young growths can be rooted in a propagating frame in mid- to late summer, or suitable pendant shoots can be layered in autumn and the resulting plants removed from their parents in spring.

AMPELOPSIS

Ampelopsis is often confused with vitis and parthenocissus for the very good reason that botanists have been lumping them together and pulling them apart for years. However, if I write quickly there is a chance that the plant I am going to mention will still be called ampelopsis by the time you come to read about it. *Ampelopsis brevipedunculata* has leaves like hop, vigorous questing stems ideal for clothing eyesores and produces quantities of small blue grapes in a good summer – they are decorative rather than delicious.

POSITION AND SOIL

The plant will grow well in ordinary soil and sun or light shade, but if fruits are to form regularly it will have to be planted against a south- or west-facing wall.

CULTIVATION

Plant in spring or autumn. Once the plant has become established problems will only be encountered in restricting, rather than encouraging, its growth. Keep the tendril-clad stems away from roofing tiles and guttering and they will perform well without endangering your property.

PRUNING AND TRAINING

Ampelopsis fastens itself to its support with coiling tendrils and if grown on a wall or fence needs wires or trellis to which it can cling. Prune only to thin out the stems which would otherwise tangle themselves together forming a thicket of growth. When trained against walls or fences, space out a good framework of stems in winter and leave the plant to grow unrestricted through summer. The following winter, when the leaves have fallen, unwanted stems can be cut out and side-shoots shortened to two or three buds. Remove shoots during the growing season only when they look like forcing their way into waste pipes or under roofing tiles.

PROPAGATION

Root cuttings of firm young growths in a propagating frame in mid- to late summer.

CALLISTEMON

Although it is hardy only in the most sheltered gardens of the south and west of England, the bottle brush tree still deserves to be grown wherever there is the slightest chance of it surviving. The narrow evergreen leaves are mundane enough, but in summer when the branches push out their cylindrical 'bottle brushes' of rich red bristles the effect is nothing short of sensational.

At least three species can usually manage to survive outdoors in mild parts. *Callistemon citrinus* and its scarlet-plumed variety 'Splendens' are perhaps the most tender types. The species will reach a height of 3–4 m (10–12 ft) and the variety only 2 m (6 ft). More reliably hardy are *C. rigidus*, deep red, 3–4 m (10–12 ft) and *C. salignus* which has yellow brushes and grows to 2 m (6 ft).

POSITION AND SOIL

The plants are not climbers but they do like the shelter of a south- or west-facing wall and the branches can be trained in to some extent or left to grow outwards – whichever you prefer or your particular situation demands. Ordinary soil suits them, but they will not tolerate chalky or wet ground. A good loam (that elusive requirement) is best of all.

CULTIVATION

Plant in spring. Although they are tender shrubs there is little you can do to protect their shoots in winter so make sure that a sheltered spot is chosen at planting time.

PRUNING AND TRAINING

Unless it is necessary to remove damaged wood, pruning should not be carried out at all. If you wish to tie branches in to the wall, horizontal wires should be strained between vine eyes fixed to the surface.

PROPAGATION

Cuttings of firm young growths can be rooted in a propagating frame in mid- to late summer.

Gamblers with sunny walls will enjoy planting the trumpet vine, *Campsis radicans* and hoping that the summer is warm enough to encourage the production of those bright trumpets.

CAMELLIA

There are several thousand varieties of camellia with single or double flowers in shades of crimson, pink, and cream through to white, which increases your chances of finding at least one that appeals to you. The majority of these varieties are derived from the species *Camellia japonica* and *C. × williamsii*; a lesser number have either *C. reticulata* or *C. sasanqua* as one parent. All are evergreen and have oval shiny leaves.

   C. × williamsii and its varieties are, I think, the best garden camellias. Their blooms are well formed, they drop as they fade (rather than turning brown on the plant) and they stand up well to British weather conditions. In time the plants will reach a height of 3 m (10 ft) and they are hardy in all but the coldest and most exposed gardens. The different varieties flower in succession from autumn to spring.

   C. japonica provides the vast bulk of garden varieties, many of which may eventually reach a height of 9 m (30 ft), though they are usually much smaller. They flower in late winter and spring and the single varieties usually have a central boss of prominent yellow-tipped stamens. The flowers of both types may be burned by frost but it is unlikely that the plants themselves will suffer.

   Recommended varieties:

C. × williamsii
'Bartley Pink'	Bright pink, single
'C. F. Coates'	Deep rose pink, single (fishtail leaves)
'Citation'	Pale pink, semi-double
'Donation'	Rich pink, semi-double
'Francis Hanger'	White, single
'J. C. Williams'	Rich pink, single
'Parkside'	Rich pink, semi-double

C. japonica
'Adolphe Audusson'	Rich red, semi-double
'Alba Plena'	White, double
'Donckelarii'	Red marbled with white, semi-double
'Flora'	White, single
'Peach Blossom'	Pale pink, semi-double
'Pink Champagne'	Pale pink, semi-double
'Tricolor'	White streaked with carmine, semi-double

POSITION AND SOIL

Camellias are frequently grown successfully in shady spots in light woodland, but they will often flower better when planted in full sun against a south- or west-facing wall. (Avoid planting them against east-facing walls for here the early morning sun can damage the flower buds by thawing them out too quickly on a frosty morning.)

The branches of the shrub may be left to spread naturally, or else tied in so that the entire framework is flat against the wall. Whichever method you choose, do make sure that the soil is not alkaline. It should be enriched with peat, well-rotted garden compost and manure so that it is spongy and moisture retentive – an essential requirement if the flower buds of the camellia are not to fall before they open. Camellias should always be planted in an acid or neutral soil, and provided that sufficient attention is paid to watering they may be grown successfully in tubs.

CULTIVATION

Plant in spring. A good mulch of well-rotted manure, leaf-mould or garden compost should be spread around the base of the plant each spring and one or two applications of diluted iron sequestrene at the same time of year. If the plants are short of iron their leaves will start to turn yellow; the iron sequestrene makes up this deficiency and your plants should soon green up again if the soil is not alkaline.

Give the soil a good soak by leaving a hose-pipe running if it shows signs of drying out. Camellias will not enjoy a drought.

PRUNING AND TRAINING

Regular pruning of camellias is not necessary. In the early years of growth, shoots may be pinched out to encourage the production of a good number of branches from near ground level, and subsequently any shoots damaged by frost can be cut back to a strong bud in spring.

Old plants that have become leggy may have their longest shoots reduced by a third in spring, and any badly placed growths can be removed at this time too.

The shoots of plants being grown against walls can be partially or entirely tied in to support wires. Those which grow straight out from the plant may have to be reduced in length or removed altogether if they encroach on a path or driveway.

PROPAGATION

Cuttings of firm young growths can be rooted in a propagating frame in summer.

CAMPSIS

The orange or red trumpets of this plant are among the most spectacular flowers to be produced by any climber. Fittingly christened the trumpet vine or trumpet creeper, campsis is a rather tender deciduous plant available in two different species. *Campsis grandiflora* can grow to 8 m (25 ft), has twining stems, pinnate leaves and clusters of orange-scarlet flowers 8 cm (3 in) across in late summer and early autumn.

C. radicans is even more vigorous, ultimately reaching 9 or 12 m (30 or 40 ft), and climbs by means of aerial roots. The pinnate leaves have more leaflets than those of *C. grandiflora* and the flowers are redder, longer and more funnel-shaped. The species also flowers in late summer and early autumn.

There is hybrid between the two species which has the rather unwieldy name of *C. × tagliabuana*, but the form of it known as 'Madame Galen' is easier to ask for and better to grow. It has salmon flowers in late summer and may prove hardier than its parents.

POSITION AND SOIL

Campsis is a sun worshipper and needs a south- or west-facing wall to do well. In sheltered gardens it will happily make itself at home over a tall tree stump or on an unproductive fruit tree. For best results the soil should be rich and moisture-retentive. Work in a good supply of well-rotted manure or garden compost at planting time.

CULTIVATION

Plant in spring. The young shoots should be tied in to the support system to make sure that they get a hold. As the plant grows it will need little assistance. Apply a thick mulch of manure or compost to the soil around the plant each spring.

PRUNING AND TRAINING

When grown against a wall, campsis should be provided with horizontal wires every 30 cm (1 ft) or so to which it can attach itself. It will usually manage to scramble through them but any wayward stems can be tied in. Trellis is a suitable alternative means of support. Space out the stems in the first year or two to form a good framework, and the plant can then be allowed to go its own way. In spring any side-shoots not needed as framework should be cut back to two or three buds – it is from these that the flowering shoots are produced. Prune every spring in this fashion, training in or shortening all shoots.

PROPAGATION

Cuttings of firm young growths can be rooted in a propagating frame in summer. Suitable stems may be layered in spring or autumn.

CARPENTERIA

Its rather tender disposition has resulted in *Carpenteria californica*, the Californian mock orange, being all too infrequently planted. But find the right situation for it and it will delight you in midsummer with a show of fragrant, wide-faced white blooms, each centred with a yellow tuft of stamens. The foliage is oval and evergreen, and the entire plant will reach a height of 2 or 2.5 m (6 or 8 ft).

POSITION AND SOIL
A south- or west-facing wall is what this plant needs to afford it maximum protection from biting winds and to expose it to the sun which it adores. A soil which is on the light side suits it best.

CULTIVATION
Plant in spring. It does not seem to be very long lived and after several years of good service it may die for no apparent reason. Propagate a few plants from your existing one to take care of this eventuality.

PRUNING AND TRAINING
Plant the bush some distance from the wall to allow it to develop a good shape: it does not need tying in. Remove one or two older branches each year, cutting them out at ground level. Allow young growths to replace them.

PROPAGATION
Take cuttings of firm young growths in summer and root them in a propagating frame (be patient; carpenteria can be tricky to root). Sow seeds under glass in spring.

CEANOTHUS

There are both deciduous and evergreen species and varieties of ceanothus, but it is the latter which are best suited to being grown against walls. All will produce their delightful blue powerpuff blooms in quantity during spring, summer or autumn. Some species are more tender than others but all should really be given a sheltered position against a south- or west-facing fence or wall. Here are just a few of the best: Ceanothus 'Autumnal Blue' is very hardy and carries its flowers in late summer and autumn; C. 'Burkwoodii' produces blooms at any time between summer and autumn; C. 'Delight' is a spring-flowering type; C. dentatus flowers in early summer; C. thyrsiflorus and C. × veitchianus are both very hardy and also flower in early summer. One or two new pink varieties are now available.

All these evergreen species have oval or rounded leaves which are often coarsely toothed and shiny, and the plants mentioned here may grow anything from 1.25–3 m (4–10 ft) tall. Although they are not climbers, most ceanothus naturally spread their branches out in the shape of a fan when grown against a wall or fence, proving that they are well suited to this type of cultivation.

POSITION AND SOIL
To give of their best ceanothus should have a sheltered spot. In very

exposed gardens the leaves may be badly browned by frost in winter and the stem tips killed off. They prefer a light, well-drained soil and sulk in shallow soil over chalk. Most thrive in seaside localities.

CULTIVATION

Plant in spring from containers – these plants resent any form of root disturbance. Mulching and feeding are unnecessary and will only give rise to lush leafy growth. In extreme drought the plants may be watered but are capable of withstanding dryness of soil to a considerable degree.

PRUNING AND TRAINING

In the early stages of training, a fanshaped framework of stems should be tied in against trellis or wires fixed to the wall or fence. As the shrub grows, new shoots should be retained to replace those which have become old and bare. Training is made easier if the shrub is planted right against the wall. Evergreen ceanothus do not require a great deal of pruning; it is sufficient to shorten the flowering shoots as the blooms fade, so encouraging the production of stems which will carry next year's blooms. *C.* 'Autumnal Blue' and *C.* 'Burkwoodii' flower in

Californian lilacs are excellent for warm and sunny walls. *Ceanothus* 'Cascade' produces its fluffy blue flowers in spring and early summer.

summer and autumn on the current year's wood, and these two varieties should be pruned in the same way as the spring-flowering types and at the same time, so that shoots will be formed during spring and early summer and flowers in late summer and autumn.

PROPAGATION

Cuttings of firm young growths may be rooted in a propagating frame from mid- to late summer.

CELASTRUS

Not a shrub for the tidy minded, celastrus makes a great sprawling mass of twining stems which in autumn are wreathed in orange capsules that burst open to reveal scarlet berries. At the same time the leaves turn bright yellow before falling. If you have an exposed garden you can rest assured that this climber is as tough as old boots and will be happy to throw its stems around an old stump or tree.

Celastrus orbiculatus is the species which fruits most reliably in this country and is the one you should choose. It can grow to a height of 9 or 12 m (30 or 40 ft) but this is governed by the height of the support. Watch out when you handle the shoots; there are thorns hidden beneath those innocent-looking leaves.

POSITION AND SOIL

Celastrus is unfussy about its position. It will thrive in full sun or partial shade, and any ordinary soil will provide all the sustenance it needs. It can be trained aganst a wall or fence, or even up a stout arch or pergola, but it looks best when allowed to scramble through a tree, over a tall stump, or even across the roof of a summerhouse. When it reaches the top of its support it casts its stems downwards where they effectively display their fruits and autumn tints.

CULTIVATION

Plant in spring or autumn. Male, female and hermaphrodite forms are available and to be sure of fruits you should plant either a male *and* female, or else make sure that you obtain a hermaphrodite.

PRUNING AND TRAINING

This is not a plant to train, and little is needed in the way of pruning. Remove any dead wood and thin the plant by cutting out a few stems completely in winter if necessary. You need plenty of space to grow it properly.

PROPAGATION

Layer suitably pendulous shoots in autumn; take cuttings of firm young growths in summer and root them in a propagating frame; sow seeds outdoors in autumn and winter.

CHAENOMELES

The Japanese quinces have suffered many changes of name at the hands of botanists, and gardeners have, not surprisingly, become confused. The names 'cydonia' and 'japonica' are still applied to what we must now call chaenomeles, and it is likely that this habit will continue for some time. To briefly set the record straight, the common quince is now *Cydonia oblonga*; all the rest are species of chaenomeles.

These ornamental quinces are first-rate deciduous garden shrubs which decorate their branches with pink, white or red blossom in winter and spring. They thrive in the open but their habit of growing wider than they are tall makes them excellent subjects for planting against a wall – especially under a window.

Chaenomeles japonica grows to between 1 and 1.5 m (3 and 5 ft) tall and has orange-red flowers in spring; *C. speciosa* flowers earlier (from late winter to spring) and has given rise to a number of good varieties with large flowers of various colours. Particularly eye-catching are 'Brilliant', scarlet; 'Moerloosii', pink and white; 'Nivalis', white; 'Phylis Moore', almond pink, semi-double; 'Simonii', rich red, semi-double, and 'Spitfire', deep red.

A cross between *C. japonica* and *C. speciosa* is C. × *superba*, and this in turn has produced some bright-flowered offspring, among the best of which are: 'Nicoline', scarlet; 'Hever Castle', pink; 'Knap Hill Scarlet', bright red flowers over a long period, and 'Rowallane', crimson. All these varieties vary in height between 1 and 3 m (3 and 10 ft). As the flowers fade they are followed by large, yellow aromatic fruits that show up well against the green foliage which emerges in spring. Enjoy an added bonus and pick the fruits when they are ripe – they make delicious quince jelly.

POSITION AND SOIL
The ornamental quinces are hardy, unfussy about soil and will tolerate being planted against walls of any aspect, though they are somewhat freer flowering in full sun.

CULTIVATION
Plant in spring or autumn, preferably from containers as the roots resent disturbance.

PRUNING AND TRAINING
Wire or trellis should be fastened to the wall to facilitate tying in of the branches. In the first few years a fan of strong growths should be trained in and all outward-growing shoots cut back to three or four buds. Subsequent pruning involves the cutting back of laterals to two or three buds immediately after flowering.

The fact that the bright quince flowers appear when there is little else to look at makes them especially valuable. *Chaenomeles × superba* 'Rowallane' has rich red flowers.

PROPAGATION
Layer suitably pendant shoots in winter/spring; cuttings of young growths can be rooted in a propagating frame in mid- to late summer.

CHIMONANTHUS

The winter sweet is a rather temperamental plant in its childhood and needs a good five years to settle in before it will think of flowering. *Chimonanthus praecox* (formerly more descriptively known as *C. fragrans*) is the only species, and its translucent yellow fringed bells hide smaller maroon ones in their centres. The blooms are sweetly scented and appear in winter when the branches are naked. There are two varieties of the species: 'Grandiflorus' has larger, deeper yellow flowers, and 'Luteus' has entirely yellow flowers that open later in winter. The leaves of all three are rather uninteresting when out of flower.

If you are determined to grow winter sweet, find it a tall and sunny wall which is rather out of the way. There it can do its own thing (it will grow up to 3 m (10 ft) tall) and you can cut some stems when they are in flower, bringing them indoors to sniff and admire.

POSITION AND SOIL

A south- or west-facing wall will protect the flowers from frost, and a good, well-drained loam will produce the best plants. However, good specimens have been grown on heavy clay and soils containing chalk.

CULTIVATION

Plant in autumn, enriching the soil with a little leaf-mould.

PRUNING AND TRAINING

Horizontal wires attached to the wall with vine eyes make the best support system. Tie in a well-spaced framework of branches as the shrub grows. Little pruning is needed and flowering is usually improved if the shrub can be left to its own devices. Stems which are thrown outwards from the wall can be removed to keep the plant tidy, and each year one or two older branches can be cut out and replaced with more youthful ones.

PROPAGATION

Layer suitably pendent stems in winter/spring; sow seeds as soon as they are ripe in a cool greenhouse or frame.

CHOISYA

Most of us garden nowadays on very small plots, so it is useful if the plants we cultivate have either a long season of flowering or else more than one pleasant attribute. The Mexican orange blossom, *Choisya ternata*, fulfils both requirements. It carries its white starry flowers in clusters in mid- and late spring, then intermittently until the end of summer, and even has the stamina to produce a few in winter if the weather is favourable. At all times of year the blooms are exquisitely fragrant. On the rare occasions when the shrub is out of flower its shiny evergreen leaves are there to be admired. Each leaf which comprises three leaflets is highly aromatic when crushed.

Choisya has no climbing tendencies at all – it just enjoys the protection afforded by a fence or wall – and it will eventually make a rounded bush 2-3 m (6–10 ft) tall, though it can be kept lower than this by pruning.

POSITION AND SOIL

Although it enjoys the warmth to be found against a south-facing wall, choisya will also do well against walls with a northerly aspect in the warmer counties. Its compromising nature is reflected in its ability to grow in a wide range of soils from heavy clays to light sands and ground which is chalky. Sheltered from searing winds it will also thrive in coastal gardens.

CULTIVATION

Plant in autumn or spring. Avoid planting choisya too close to the wall; it will make a better-shaped shrub if planted 45–60 cm (1½–2 ft) away.

PRUNING AND TRAINING

Cut out any frost-damaged stems in spring and remove very old growths when the plants become overcrowded. Reduce the length of all the stems by 15 or 30 cm (6 or 12 in) immediately after flowering. Apart from ensuring the production of new growth this pruning will encourage a second flush of flowers later in the year.

PROPAGATION

Cuttings of firm young growths can be rooted in a propagating frame in summer.

CLEMATIS

Variously known as virgin's bower and the queen of climbers, clematis is one of the most beautiful and indispensable of garden plants. Large- and small-flowered varieties in shades of pink, purple, magenta, red, yellow, cream, blue and white abound, and there are several with double blooms. Most are deciduous (though one or two are evergreen) and the majority are hardy enough to survive bad winters even in exposed gardens. They climb to between 3 and 5 m (10 and 15 ft) high (though the vigorous *Clematis montana* may reach 9 m (30 ft) or more) and the plants cling by means of their twining leaf stalks which act rather like tendrils.

The vast number of varieties available is quite bewildering. Here I will mention just 25 of the best in the hope that a least a handful of them will offer you the right coloured flowers at the right time. The number given after each variety refers to the way in which it is best pruned (for details see under pruning and training, p. 35.)

GOOD GARDEN CLEMATIS

C. alpina	Nodding, blue quartered bells carried singly from the leaf axils in mid and late spring (1)
C. armandii	Evergreen, slightly tender, needs a warm wall where its clusters of small white flowers will release their sweet fragrance in mid and late spring (1)
'Barbara Dibley'	Large magenta flowers in late spring, early summer and again in early autumn (2)

'Barbara Jackman'

Large lavender blue flowers, each sepal with a magenta stripe down the middle in late spring, early summer and in early autumn (2)

'Comtesse de Bouchaud'

Large rose pink flowers from early to late summer (3)

'Countesse of Lovelace'

Large pale blue flowers (double at the beginning of the season, single later in the year) in late spring, early summer and again in late summer (2)

'Elsa Späth'

Large lavender blue flowers in late spring, early summer and again in late summer (2)

'Ernest Markham'

Large magenta flowers from early summer to early autumn (3)

'Etoile Rose'

Deep rose pink quartered bells with paler edges from early summer to early autumn (3)

C. florida 'Sieboldii'

Small creamy-white flowers, each with a large central boss of purple stamens from early to late summer (2)

'Gipsy Queen'

Large violet-purple flowers from midsummer to early autumn (3)

'Hagley Hybrid'

Large shell pink flowers from early summer to early autumn (3)

C. × jackmanii 'Superba'

Large violet-purple flowers from midsummer to early autumn (3)

'Lasurstern'

Large lavender blue flowers with wavy-edged sepals in late spring, early summer and early autumn (2)

C. macropetala

Nodding double flowers of lavender blue and white in late spring and early summer (1)

'Marie Boisselot'

Large flowers of the palest pink becoming white, from late spring to mid-autumn (2)

'Mrs Cholmondeley'

Large lavender-blue flowers from late spring to late summer (3)

C. montana

Very vigorous plant with masses of small, white, fragrant, four-petalled flowers in late spring and early summer. C. montana rubens is pale pink (1)

'Nelly Moser'

Large pale pink flowers, each sepal having a central carmine stripe, in late spring, early summer and again in late summer and early autumn (2)

C. orientalis	Bright yellow bells with thick sepals, followed by fluffy seedheads, in late summer and early autumn (3)
'Perle d'Azur'	Large pale blue flowers from early to late summer (3)
C. tangutica	Similar to *C. orientalis* but flowers rather larger in late summer and early autumn; more spectacular fluffy seedheads, are produced (3)
'Ville de Lyon'	Large carmine red flowers from midsummer to mid-autumn (3)
'Vyvyan Pennell'	Large bluish-mauve double flowers in late spring and early summer, paler single blooms carried later in early autumn (2)
'W. E. Gladstone'	Large lavender-blue flowers from early summer to early autumn (2)

POSITION AND SOIL

Clematis always look best if their 'legs' are covered up, so if you grow them at the foot of a wall or fence, plant a small shrub in front of them to mask the bare, uninteresting stem and to prevent the soil from being dried out by the sun. Some clematis will certainly tolerate shade, but most like their shoots and flowers in the sun and their roots in cool, moist soil. Chalky ground will be enjoyed if it is enriched with manure or compost.

To my eye, clematis really look their best when planted at the foot of a tree or among other shrubs. In these situations their stems can ramble through the stronger branches of their neighbours and their flowers can be seen to advantage. *C. macropetala* performs well in tubs and urns if the soil is not allowed to dry out too much, and *C. montana* and its varieties can be used to cover unsightly garages and sheds. Large-flowered varieties can be trained up poles, arches and pergolas.

CULTIVATION

Plant in spring or autumn. If the clematis is to be trained up a tree or through a shrub, plant it 45 cm (18 in) from its host and bridge the gap with a bamboo cane up which the young clematis can climb. Enrich the soil with well-rotted manure or garden compost and lay a mulch of similar material around the plant each spring. If another shrub cannot be planted in front of a wall-trained clematis, lay a flagstone or two over the soil to prevent it from drying out. Set the plant 30–45 cm (1–1½ ft) from the brickwork – the soil right against the wall can become very dry.

A mysterious fungus disease known as clematis wilt will sometimes

Large-flowered clematises such as 'Lasurstern' look well when trained up and over old tree stumps.

attack plants without warning causing leaves and shoots to collapse and wither. Cut out any affected stems and water the soil around the plant with benomyl. In severe cases it may be necessary to cut the plant right back to ground level.

If the first flush of flowers is green and poorly coloured, give the plant a dose of diluted liquid tomato fertilizer each week in late spring and early summer – this should put matters right.

One final note on cultivation: be patient. Some varieties take quite a while to settle down and flower well. Once they feel at home they will amply repay your earlier kindnesses.

PRUNING AND TRAINING

Pruning is necessary with most clematis to ensure that they produce the maximum amount of flowering wood at a level where the blooms can be appreciated. In the list of varieties each plant is numbered according to the way in which it should be pruned. The methods are as follows:

1) Prune these varieties only if they are becoming overcrowded and too large for the space allotted to them. Remove shoots that have

flowered as soon as the blooms fade and cut out any dead wood. New stems can be trained in to take the place of the old ones.

2) Remove damaged or dead stems and cut back the rest to a pair of strong buds. Prune these varieties in late winter and early spring.

3) The varieties in this group flower later and therefore have more time to produce flowering shoots. For this reason they can be pruned quite hard, to within 1 m (3 ft) or so of ground level. Cut back each stem to a healthy pair of buds in late winter and early spring and remove any dead or damaged stems entirely.

The stems will find plenty to cling to if the plants are grown among shrubs or through trees. On walls and fences they should be provided with wires or trellis-work. On arches and pergolas they will need tying in. Take care to keep the stems of *C. montana* away from gutters and roofs or they may block pipes and lift slates. Trimmed back each year they can be kept in check.

PROPAGATION

Suitable mature stems can be layered in summer, and cuttings of young growths can be rooted in a propagating frame at the same time of year. Clematis cuttings are prepared rather differently from those of other shrubs (see the chapter on propagation). Seeds of the species may be sown in a cool greenhouse or frame in spring.

CLIANTHUS

The lobster claw, *Clianthus puniceus*, is a shrub only for gamblers. A native of New Zealand it needs a warm wall and a lot of luck to survive. Having said that, if you are prepared to take a chance with it and you succeed it will more than repay your patience and courage. Its ferny fronds lie flat against the wall when it is tied in and its peculiarly shaped scarlet flowers drip luxuriantly from the stems in summer. Clianthus is semi-evergreen (it will lose some of its leaves in winter) and will reach a height of about 2–2.5 m (6–8 ft). The white form *albus* is not so spectacular as the straight species.

POSITION AND SOIL

A south- or west-facing wall is essential, and if you live in one of the more exposed counties you have only a slight chance of getting the plant through the winter. A light soil is preferred.

CULTIVATION

Plant in spring. This plant does not grow very tall and so you may be able to protect its tender stems in winter by covering them with bracken or straw held in place by wire or plastic netting.

PRUNING AND TRAINING

Although it does not climb, clianthus lends itself to being planted against a wall because its branches arch gently and can easily be tied in to horizontal wires or trellis-work. Pruning consists of cutting out frost-damaged growth in spring, and reducing the number of old stems when they start to compete with one another. In the early years the main shoots can be pinched out in spring to encourage branching.

PROPAGATION

Seeds can be sown in a warm greenhouse in spring and cuttings of firm young growths rooted in a propagating frame in summer.

COBAEA

Although they need to be raised afresh each year, annual climbers are nevertheless well worth growing. The cup and saucer vine, *Cobaea scandens*, is one of the quaintest. From midsummer until the frosts of autumn it decorates its tendril-clad stems with large bells which are greenish-white at first, turning to rich purple as they age. Long white stamens with upturned ends stand out well against the darkened blooms. The plant will grow rapidly in a favourable spot, reaching 3 m (10 ft) and more in a single season.

POSITION AND SOIL

Planted at the foot of a sunny wall, fence, pergola or arch in good but not over-rich soil, cobaea will perform well. On patios and balconies it can be grown in a tub equipped with a tall tripod of canes.

CULTIVATION

Harden off the plants before planting them out in late spring or early summer when danger of frost is past. Aviod making the soil too rich at planting time or leafy growth will be produced at the expense of flowers. An occasional feed with diluted liquid tomato fertilizer during summer will encourage the production of flowers.

PRUNING AND TRAINING

On a flat wall or fence horizontal wires or trellis should be provided to give the plant something to cling to. Stray stems can be twined around the supports when necessary. Cobaea is really a perennial but it is cut to the ground by autumn frosts and so best treated as an annual.

PROPAGATION

Sow seeds in a warm greenhouse/frame in spring.

CONVOLVULUS

Put aside the idea that all plants with the name convolvulus are as bad as that pernicious garden horror known as bindweed. The convolvulus I am about to describe has none of its embarassing relation's bad habits; on the contrary, it needs a little cosseting if it is to do well. *Convolvulus cneorum* is one of our best silver-foliaged plants and I have sneaked it into these pages for the legitimate reason that it thrives best at the foot of a warm wall, and also because it deserves to be more widely planted.

It will no more climb than fly – it contents itself with making rounded or rather sprawling mounds which, due to the silky hairs on its leaves, glisten in the sunlight. The flowers are produced erratically from early summer onwards and are smaller, daintier replicas of those white trumpets possessed by the weed, except that on this plant they are pink on the reverse. The maximum height of this convolvulus is 1 m (3 ft) and its leaves are retained all the year round.

POSITION AND SOIL
A light, well-drained loam at the foot of a south- or west-facing wall will grow the best plants.

CULTIVATION
Plant in spring. The plant will survive relatively mild winters but may

The orange peel clematis, *Clematis orientalis*, has thick-petalled yellow lantern flowers followed by fluffy seedheads.

be killed off by severe and prolonged frosts. Safeguard against loss by rooting a few cuttings each year to act as replacements. If covered with bracken or straw as winter protection the plant may rot.

PRUNING AND TRAINING
Cut out frost-damaged growth in spring and remove any old and top-heavy shoots at the same time.

PROPAGATION
Cuttings of firm young growths can be rooted in a propagating frame in summer.

CORONILLA

There are two species of coronilla which, although they are not climbers, are excellent shrubs for planting at the foot of a warm wall due to their tender disposition. *Coronilla glauca* is the more obviously attractive of the two, carrying bright yellow, fragrant pea-shaped flowers among its finely cut blue-grey foliage at any time from early spring to early winter. *C. emerus*, the scorpion senna, is deciduous (*C. glauca* is evergreen), has gracefully arching stems clad in green foilage and carries its bright yellow flowers throughout the summer. Both plants can apparently reach a height of 2.5 m (8 ft) and more but specimens taller than 1.25 m (4 ft) are not common.

POSITION AND SOIL
A south- or west-facing wall will give them the sun and protection they need, and a rather light, well-drained soil suits them best.

CULTIVATION
Plant in spring. In hard winters the foliage of *C. glauca* may be burned, the shoot tips killed or the entire plant wiped out. Root a few cuttings which can be kept to act as replacements in the event of fatality.

PRUNING AND TRAINING
One or two of the oldest stems can be removed entirely each spring; frost-burned shoots of *C. glauca* can be cut out at the same time. To encourage new shoots, cut back old plants of *C. emerus* quite hard.

PROPAGATION
Cuttings of firm young growths can be rooted in a propagating frame in summer.

COTONEASTER

There are many cotoneasters and most of them are too vigorous and spreading to be planted against walls. But there are several which do lend themselves to this type of culture by virtue of their individual habits. *Cotoneaster microphyllus* and *C. horizontalis* might, at first glance, appear to be rather alike, but the first named is evergreen and the latter deciduous. *C. horizontalis* produces stiff, arching stems, each one pushing out sideshoots at regular intervals in a fishbone pattern. It will usually reach a height of 2 m (6 ft) or so against a wall and its stems carry tiny dark green leaves in summer and scarlet berries in winter. *C. microphyllus* is dwarfer and suitable for planting on banks or to cover the lower part of a wall. The dark green glossy leaves show off the scarlet berries well in winter. *C. salicifolius* is a more vigorous evergreen with willow-shaped leaves carried on gently arching stems. Clusters of red berries are borne in winter and the plant may reach a height of 3 m (10 ft) or more. All three species have white flowers in summer.

POSITION AND SOIL

Cotoneasters are useful plants for they will thrive in sun or shade and in any soil.

CULTIVATION

Plant in autumn and winter. Once planted they will need little attention.

PRUNING AND TRAINING

Little, if any, pruning is required. Take the secateurs to these plants in spring only if they are outgrowing the space available and then simply remove a few branches entirely. Tie the main stems of *C. horizontalis* and *C. salicifolius* to horizontal wires attached to the wall.

PROPAGATION

Sow seeds outdoors in spring; cuttings of firm young growths can be rooted in a frame in summer.

CUCURBITA

Two of our favourite edible cucurbits, the marrow and the pumpkin, have a smaller but more vividly coloured relation, the gourd, which is an amusing and decorative annual climber. All three plants are derived from *Cucurbita pepo* but the gourds are grown strictly for their ornamental value and not for food.

Most seedsmen offer a mixed strain, though a few do go in for peculiar varieties with names like 'Turk's Cap', 'Hercules Club' and 'Japanese Nest Egg'. The mixed selection is likely to include plants with orange, green, yellow and white fruits, many of them parti-coloured and varying in form from the spherical to the pear-shaped. A good many will possess highly unpleasant looking warts too!

Left on their own the plants will sprawl, but can easily be trained up pergolas and trellises to a height of 3 m (10 ft) or more.

POSITION AND SOIL

A sunny spot is necessary if the plants are to produce an abundance of fruits. They are greedy too and like a rich soil which is not likely to dry out in summer. Gourds are easy plants to cultivate in tubs, provided that they are not kept short of moisture, and a tripod of 2 m (6 ft) bamboo canes will give them sufficient support.

CULTIVATION

Harden off the plants prior to planting out in spring when danger of frost is past. The site should be laced with plenty of well-rotted manure or garden compost before planting. Give the soil a good soak whenever it looks like drying out through the summer, and as the fruits start to swell a fortnightly liquid feed will give them a boost. In late summer as soon as the fruits are fully developed and are beginning to dry out they can be cut from the plant and the drying process completed indoors. When dry and hard they can be painted with clear varnish and their bright colours enjoyed through the winter months.

PRUNING AND TRAINING

No pruning is necessary, though rampant stems can be cut out if they outgrow the space available. Tie the shoots in to the support system as they extend.

PROPAGATION

Seeds can be sown in pots of seed compost during spring and germinated in a warm greenhouse. Alternatively, sow them outdoors where they are to grow in late spring, protecting the young seedlings with a pane of glass or a cloche in the early stages of growth.

CYTISUS

Most brooms are happy in a sunny spot in the open garden but *Cytisus battandieri* looks particularly good when grown against a wall. The stems and silvery leaves are larger and more robust than those of other brooms and the bright yellow pineapple-scented flowers are carried in closely packed cockades during early and midsummer. Given a warm and sunny spot the plant will eventually reach 3 or 4 m (10 or 12 ft).

POSITION AND SOIL

Although it can withstand most winters in the southern counties, this cytisus is safer if planted in the shelter of a south- or west-facing wall. It prefers ordinary well-drained soil but it will also tolerate clay and chalk – although on the latter brooms are likely to be short lived. In coastal gardens it should be sheltered from strong winds.

CULTIVATION

Plant in autumn and winter. Container-grown plants are the best to

Plant the Moroccan broom against a sunny wall and you will be able to enjoy its bright yellow pineapple-scented flowers in summer.

buy as brooms dislike any form of root disturbance.

PRUNING AND TRAINING
Little training is needed with this plant as it is strong enough to support itself. As to pruning, remove only those stems which grow straight out from the wall, so causing an obstruction, and one or two of the oldest ones each winter – allowing young vigorous shoots to take their place.

PROPAGATION
Seeds can be sown in pots of seed compost in spring and germinated in a cold frame. Pot up the seedlings when large enough and grow them on in containers until planting time.

ECCREMOCARPUS

Eccremocarpus scaber, the Chilean glory flower, is a dainty half-hardy climber which has ferny foliage and clusters of scarlet or orange tubular flowers from summer to autumn. Its tendrils help it to climb and it may reach 3 or 4 m (10 or 12 ft) in one season.

POSITION AND SOIL
If it is planted among shrubs or at the foot of a tree its stems will inquisitively work their way among the nearby branches, eventually wreathing them in flowers. On warm walls and arches in the sun it is equally at home and its rate of growth rapid. A light, well-drained soil suits it best.

Even with easy-to-grow plants like forsythia it's worth choosing a good form such as 'Nymans' to make sure of a bright spring show.

CULTIVATION

Plant in spring when danger of frost is past. A little well-rotted manure or compost worked into the soil at planting time will give the plant the energy it needs to cover the support system. The growth may be cut back to the ground by autumn and winter frosts but shoots will often emerge at ground level the following spring. Protect the roots and crown of the plant in winter with a layer of sharp sand topped up with bracken or straw. If you live in a particularly cold locality the plant may be best treated as a half-hardy annual and raised afresh from seed each spring. Healthy young seedlings planted out in late spring will flower during the same summer.

PRUNING AND TRAINING

Cut out all dead wood each spring when the new shoots are emerging. Provide horizontal wires or trellis-work when the plant is being grown against a wall or fence and tie in any wayward stems.

PROPAGATION

Seed can be sown in a warm greenhouse in spring, the young plants potted up and planted out when there is no danger of frost.

ESCALLONIA

The glossy evergreen leaves and small red, pink or white flowers of escallonia combine to make it an excellent garden shrub. Some varieties take more readily than others to being cultivated against a wall, but with a little training few of them present any difficulty.

The shrub is hardy in most parts of the country but it may be severely cut back in hard winters and so the protection given by a wall can be a lifesaver.

Escallonia macrantha is one of the best species for wall training. It will reach 3 m (10 ft), has gummy aromatic foliage and clusters of rosy-red flowers. Other varieties well worth growing in this fashion are : 'Apple Blossom', 1.25 m (4 ft), pink and white; 'Crimson Spire', 2 m (6 ft), crimson; 'Donard Seedling', 2.5 m (8 ft), pink in bud, white when open; 'Edinensis', 2 m (6 ft), deep pink in bud, shell pink when open; 'Langleyensis', 2.5 m (8 ft), rose pink. All flower in summer.

POSITION AND SOIL

All the varieties mentioned will enjoy a position against a south- or west-facing wall and *E. macrantha* will grow on those with a northerly or easterly aspect. Light, well-drained soils are preferred, but clay and chalky ground are also tolerated. All varieties are very much at home in seaside gardens.

CULTIVATION

Plant in spring or autumn. Escallonias usually thrive and flower best in soil which has not been enriched with manure or fertilizer.

PRUNING AND TRAINING

Tie in the main stems in the first few years after planting to produce a well-shaped framework of growth. Horizontal wires attached to the wall with vine eyes make the best supports. Pruning consists of shortening back all flower-bearing stems growing directly out from the wall as soon as the flowers fade. Remove any dead or weak shoots at the same time.

PROPAGATION

Cuttings of firm young shoots can be rooted in a propagating frame in summer; suitably pendulous stems can be layered in spring, severed from the parent plant in autumn and planted out on their own.

FORSYTHIA

Judging by the yellow haze to be seen in ninety-nine out of a hundred British gardens every spring, forsythia is one of the most popular garden plants. Most species and varieties are fine in the open – indeed they are as tough as old boots – but due to its rambling habit *Forsythia suspensa* does extremely well on walls and fences. It can reach a staggering 10 m (30 ft) in this situation and carries its pale yellow four-petalled bells on slender stems in early and mid-spring. The variety 'Nymans' has purplish stems that contrast well with the flowers, and on both this and *F. suspensa* the foliage is a pleasant green.

POSITION AND SOIL

A wall of any aspect and a wide range of soils will be found amenable by this accommodating shrub.

CULTIVATION

Plant in autumn. A mulch of well-rotted manure or compost should be spread around the plant each spring.

PRUNING AND TRAINING

In the first few years of growth tie in a well-spaced framework of young stems to the horizontal wires attached to the wall. Pruning should be carried out immediately after flowering. It is easy to turn a forsythia into a mass of unsightly stubby stems. Avoid this by pruning only when absolutely necessary to thin out the shrub and prevent it encroaching where it is not wanted. Cut back completely those flowered stems which are growing out from the wall unless they can be effectively tied in. Remove one or two of the oldest branches every couple of years to allow young ones to take their place.

PROPAGATION

Cuttings of firm young growths can be rooted in a propagating frame in summer; mature young stems can be layered in autumn and removed from the plant a year later.

FREMONTODENDRON

A few years ago the botanists played one of their games with a plant known as *Fremontia californica* and extended its name to *Fremontodendron californicum* – a merciful change for gardeners since the two are at least vaguely recognizable as the same thing. Apart from the change of name the only thing I can find to complain about is that it is hardy only in sheltered spots and milder gardens – something you would expect of a native of California. Give it a warm wall, though, and you stand a good chance of enjoying its large yellow flowers throughout the summer. Its leaves are evergreen (though a few may be lost in hard winters), three-lobed and maple like and the plant will eventually reach 3 m (10 ft) or more.

POSITION AND SOIL

A south- or west-facing wall is essential if the plant is to do well, and a light, well-drained soil suits it best. It will do well on chalky soil too.

CULTIVATION

Plant in spring. Fremontodendrons resent root disturbance so plant out pot-grown specimens.

PRUNING AND TRAINING
Tie in and space out the stems on a framework of horizontal wires as they grow. Prune in spring, removing only those stems killed by frost.
PROPAGATION
Seeds can be sown in a warm greenhouse in spring; cuttings of firm young growths can be rooted in a propagating frame in summer.

GARRYA

The silk tassel bush is a good plant to choose if your garden is short of items of interest in the winter. Its dark evergreen leaves show off to perfection the long grey-green catkins which emerge at any time from late autumn to late winter. Male and female catkins are carried on separate plants in the species most commonly grown, *Garrya elliptica*. The male plant has the larger tassels but those of the female are decorative too. 'James Roof' is one of the best varieties. The shrub has a fairly upright habit and may reach 4 m (12 ft) or more.

POSITION AND SOIL
A wall of any aspect will suit this plant (it is just a little tender and so enjoys the protection a wall affords) and it is tolerant of a wide range of soils from light sand to clay and those containing chalk. However, the best plants will be produced on well-drained soils in a sunny situation. It is a good wall shrub for seaside gardens.

CULTIVATION
Plant in spring or autumn. Plant out specimens which have been grown in pots; they resent root disturbance.

PRUNING AND TRAINING
Pinch the plant in its early stages of growth to encourage the production of several stems close to ground level. These can be spaced out and tied in to horizontal wires at planting time. The plant can then be left to grow unchecked and untrained, with just the larger branches being tied in for stability. When the plant encroaches on a path or drive, any branches coming straight out from the wall can be cut back immediately after flowering.

PROPAGATION
Cuttings of firm young growths can be rooted in a propagating frame in summer; suitably pendant branches can be layered in autumn.

HEDERA

If you think that ivy is a rather dull plant with boring dark green leaves, think again. There are lots of varieties offering a wide choice of leaf shape and variegation to add brightness to your garden when most plants are bare of foliage. *Hedera helix* is the species with small leaves and the most varieties. It clings by means of aerial roots and so needs no support other than a surface up which to climb. When it reaches the top of its host, be it a wall or tree, it produces different foliage along with small greenish flowers which are followed by black berries. As to its height, this ivy will undoubtedly reach the top of whatever it is planted against. Some of the best varieties are:

'Brokamp'   Green in summer turning bronze in winter
'Buttercup'   Young leaves bright yellow, becoming green with age
'Chicago'   Green leaves stained with purple
'Cristata'   Green wavy-edged leaves
'Glacier'   Small grey-green leaves edged with white
'Gold Heart'   Dark green leaves with a bright yellow central blotch
'Green Ripple'   Mid-green leaves with extra-long tapering lobes
'Sagittifolia'   Dark green leaves with pointed lobes

There are two ivies with much larger leaves and more rambling habits of growth. *H. colchica* is most frequently grown around pillars and posts; the green, grey and creamy yellow variety *dentata variegata* is the most popular. Slightly less hardy is *H. canariensis variegata* (also known as 'Gloire de Marengo') which has a white variegation. Due to its greater hardiness the former is the better choice for outdoor planting.

POSITION AND SOIL

Ivies will grow *on* anything and *in* anything. They are especially decorative on walls and will keep your house warm and dry (even if they do play host to spiders and sparrows). On brick or stone house walls they are no problem at all if properly pruned, but I would avoid planting them against walls clad in pebbledash for they can – if allowed to become too thick and heavy – pull off the surface against which they are growing in one big sheet.

They do no harm when grown up trees, provided that the trees are healthy and the ivy is restricted to the trunk and main branches, being clipped out of the twiggy, leafy areas. Over old stumps ivies look particularly at home and can make a pleasing feature out of an eyesore. Poles, arches and pergolas make suitable hosts too, as do hazel or wattle hurdles used as garden dividers.

CULTIVATION

Plant in spring or autumn at the foot of intended supports. Ivies transplanted from pots will establish themselves quickest. A solution of manure and water painted on to the wall will encourage the ivy's aerial roots to cling.

PRUNING AND TRAINING

In the early years no pruning will be necessary for the plants will be extending themselves rather than thickening up their growth. After a few years when stems and leaves have become more densely packed the plants should be clipped back with shears so that their 'mat' of growth is made lighter. Carry out this pruning in mid- or late spring. No training is necessary except on stumps, posts, pergolas and arches where the stems may have to be tied to the support in the early stages of growth, that is, until the plants have established themselves.

PROPAGATION

Cuttings of firm young growths can be rooted in a propagating frame is summer; suitably pendent growths can be layered at any time of year.

HUMULUS

The hop, apart from being a delightful ingredient of beer, is also a delightful garden plant. Two species are grown: the common hop, *Humulus lupulus*, and the Japanese hop, *H. japonicus*. Both will grow to around 5 m (15 ft) and have varieties with colourful foliage. *H. lupulus aureus* has the same finely cut, almost maple-like leaves as the straight species but they are a rich acid yellow. The plant is a perennial but its rambling tracery of leafy stems is cut down to the ground by frosts in autumn. *H. japonicus variegatus* offers leaves of a similar shape but this time splashed with white. It is less hardy than its relative and, although it may survive the winter if protected, it is usually grown as an annual. The pouch-like fruits are carried in tight clusters and dangle gracefully from the stems in summer.

POSITION AND SOIL

The hop loves sun so give it a sunny wall, pergola, post or arch over which to ramble. Over trees and stumps it also looks at home. Enrich the soil with well-rotted manure or garden compost before planting.

CULTIVATION

Plant in spring *(H. japonicus* when danger of frost is past). Mulch with manure or compost each spring and water the soil well in dry weather.

PRUNING AND TRAINING

Attach trellis-work to walls to give the plants something to hold on to, and tie in the young stems as they grow to introduce them to their support system – this also applies to plants grown on arches, pergolas and posts. After this initial help they should manage on their own. Cut away dead growth in winter.

PROPAGATION

Divide plants of *H. lupulus* in spring; sow seeds of both kinds in a warm greenhouse in spring and harden off the young plants before planting out when frost danger is past.

HYDRANGEA

While most hydrangeas form rounded bushes with no climbing tendencies at all, there are several species which are well-equipped for ascending walls and trees. Most popular of these is *Hydrangea petiolaris*. Its brown, peeling stems are furnished with aerial roots rather like those of ivy and it presses itself hard against its support, needing no additional framework to assist it in the upward climb. The leaves are green and deciduous and the white flowers are carried in large heads in early summer. This is a vigorous plant which will grow to a height of 15 m (50 ft) or more in a suitable situation.

POSITION AND SOIL
Walls of any aspect suit this hydrangea but it is particularly valuable against those of a northerly or easterly aspect. It is even more at home clambering over an old tree stump or even through a tree, where it will do no harm if restricted to the trunk and main branches. A good, well-drained soil will grow the best plants, so the addition of a little well-rotted manure or garden compost at planting time is advisable.

CULTIVATION
Plant in spring or autumn. A spring mulch of manure or compost will give the plants a much-needed boost.

PRUNING AND TRAINING
Only in the early stages will the plant need encouragement to climb. For the first year the stems should be tied to the intended support. Little pruning is required. It is sufficient simply to remove unwanted stems that grow away from the wall or tree trunk. These can be cut out as soon as they are seen in summer.

PROPAGATION
Cuttings of firm young growths can be rooted in a propagating frame in summer.

IPOMOEA

Without a doubt the morning glory is one of the most beautiful of annual climbers. Right through the summer it decorates its twining stems with pointed green leaves and brightly coloured trumpets of sky blue, rosy red or blue and white. The varieties are derived from *Ipomoea tricolor* and some of the best are: 'Heavenly Blue', sky blue with a white throat; 'Scarlet O'Hara', rosy red with a white throat, and 'Flying

Saucers', blue and white striped. All will reach a height of about 3 m (10 ft).

POSITION AND SOIL

A warm, sunny wall and soil enriched with a little fertilizer and manure will produce the best plants. Morning glories will also grow well in tubs of John Innes potting compost No. 2 if kept well supplied with water in summer.

CULTIVATION

Plant out in late spring when danger of frost is past. Fortnightly feeding with liquid tomato fertilizer through the summer will encourage flower production.

PRUNING AND TRAINING

No pruning is necessary, for this annual will be killed by the autumn frosts. Tie the shoots in to the support system in the early stages – they will soon take hold and romp away. Trellis-work or wire netting should be attached to walls and smooth fences where this climber is to be trained. In tubs, provide a tripod of bamboo canes for support.

PROPAGATION

Seeds can be sown in a warm greenhouse in spring. The young plants are then potted up and hardened off before being planted out. It is sometimes recommended that seeds are soaked for 24 hours prior to sowing. I have never found this necessary but if difficulty is encountered in germinating the seed it may be worth trying.

ITEA

It is sad that *Itea ilicifolia* is not more widely grown, for it has some valuable attributes. Its foliage is glossy, evergreen and rather like holly in appearance except that it is not so spiny, but its flowers are its main attraction. Opening from late summer onwards they are greenish-white, fragrant and carried on long, pendulous tails, well displayed against the green leaves. The only disadvantage of the shrub is its tenderness, for it needs a warm wall in a sheltered garden if it is to survive our worst winters. However, gardeners in the south or west who can offer such a situation should be tempted to try this worthy wall plant. It will reach a height of 3 m (10 ft) or so and is an upright grower rather than a climber.

POSITION AND SOIL

A sheltered wall in sun or partial shade will suit it, and good, moisture-retentive loam will produce the best plants.

CULTIVATION

Plant in spring. Mulch each spring with manure/garden compost.

PRUNING AND TRAINING

Tie in the main stems to horizontal wires attached to the wall. Regular pruning is not necessary but one or two old and weak branches can be cut out each year and strong new stems tied in to replace them.

PROPAGATION

Cuttings of firm young growths can be rooted in a propagating frame in summer; suckers can be removed and transplanted in autumn.

JASMINUM

Quite a few jasmines can be grown in the garden but most of them are not reliably hardy. The two I mention here, however, should give little cause for concern if planted in the right place. *Jasminum nudiflorum*, the winter jasmine, will stand whatever the weather has to offer, so you need not worry about its hardiness. From late autumn to late winter its bright yellow flowers sprout from the arching bare branches bringing colour at a time when it is most welcome. The plant is not a climber but grows well against a wall, eventually reaching 4 m (12 ft) or slightly more. *J. officinale*, the common jasmine, *is* a climber and its twining stems will reach 6 m (20 ft). It is semi-evergreen and has fragrant white

Although in really cold gardens *Fremontodendron californicum* may suffer from frost damage, elsewhere it can usually be relied on to survive even quite chilly winters.

flowers from early summer to early autumn. Grow both these varieties and you can bank on flowers for eight months of the year.

POSITION AND SOIL

The winter jasmine will thrive against any wall, even one which faces north, and is particularly useful for brightening a dull corner. It is tolerant of a wide range of soils from sand and clay to those containing chalk. The common jasmine is most at home when given an old tree to scramble through, but it can still be trained up trellis-work against a sunny wall. Give this species a warm and sheltered spot in cold gardens for it is not so hardy as its relative. A good loam is most to its liking.

CULTIVATION

Plant in autumn. A little well-rotted manure or garden compost worked into the soil at planting time will benefit both species.

PRUNING AND TRAINING

The common jasmine needs little in the way of pruning and training. Once introduced to its support it will soon romp away and only when it is in danger of becoming severely overcrowded should one or two of the oldest stems be removed completely. The winter jasmine, on the other hand, should be attacked annually with the secateurs to prevent it from becoming a dense mattress of dead stems. In the first few years tie in the shoots to form a fan against horizontal wires attached to the wall. Subsequently the shoots from these branches will arch outwards and downwards and it is on these growths that the plant will flower the following winter. As soon as flowering is over, cut these shoots hard back to suitable buds which will give rise to new shoots. Really old and gnarled stems can be cut out completely and replaced with strong new ones.

PROPAGATION

Cuttings of firm young growths can be rooted in a propagating frame in late summer; suitably pendant stems can be layered in spring.

KERRIA

Kerria japonica, the Jew's mallow, is wisely most frequently grown in its double form 'Pleniflora'. The miniature yellow chrysanthemum-like blooms are dotted along bright green stems in mid- and late spring and are closely followed by pointed green leaves. The plant will grow to 3 m (10 ft) against a wall where it looks most effective, its wiry stems remaining green throughout the winter.

POSITION AND SOIL

This really is an accommodating shrub which will put up with many different soils and a position against a wall or fence in sun or shade.

CULTIVATION
Plant in autumn. Pruning is quite brutal so apply a spring mulch of well-rotted manure or garden compost to encourage the production of new stems.

PRUNING AND TRAINING
Tie in the largest stems to horizontal wires attached to the wall with vine eyes. Cut out at ground level a good number of flowering stems each year when the blooms have faded, so leaving a thin framework which will be added to by new shoots through the summer.

PROPAGATION
Cuttings of firm young growths can be rooted in a propagating frame in summer; suckers can be removed and transplanted in autumn.

LABURNUM

Before you question my sanity let me point out that laburnum is *not* grown as a wall plant. It does look stunning though when its branches are tied to a metal pergola with rounded arches. Here it can be used to form a tunnel that drips with a breath-taking cascade of bright yellow pea-like blooms in late spring and early summer. *Laburnum alpinum, L. anagyroides* and *L. × watereri* 'Vossii' are all suitable, but the last named has the longest tassels of flower. Visit the Royal Botanic Gardens at Kew, Barnsley House in Gloucestershire or Bodnant Garden near Colwyn Bay and sample the effect of this magical feature yourself.

The only real disadvantage of these deciduous trees is the fact that their leaves, flowers and seeds are all poisonous if eaten and therefore a potential danger to small children.

POSITION AND SOIL
A wide range of soils will be tolerated but avoid waterlogged ones. Choose a position in full sun.

CULTIVATION
Plant in autumn. Enrich the soil with well-rotted manure or garden compost.

PRUNING AND TRAINING
The pergola can be made from steel arches set 2 m (6 ft) apart which are linked with heavy gauge wire or with steel rods. In either case the structure should be made as strong as possible for it will be in position for many years and will have to carry a considerable weight. Plant the young laburnum bushes (these are better than trees for several stems will arise at ground level) at 3 m (10 ft) intervals along either side of the pergola and tie in the stems – spacing them out evenly – on the wires or metal rods which should be positioned at 60 cm (2 ft) intervals over the

Hung where its catkins can be illuminated at night by a wall lamp, *Garrya elliptica* is transformed from being rather a dreary shrub to one of great spectacle.

pergola. Each year the long shoots required to extend the framework of branches should be tied in and side-shoots shortened to two or three buds in early winter. If larger branches have to be removed for any reason, cut them out in late summer when the cut surface will not bleed so readily as it would in spring.

PROPAGATION

Seeds can be sown outdoors in spring (after soaking them in warm water for an hour); suitable branches can be taken down to the soil and layered in spring or autumn.

LATHYRUS

Few people can be unaware of the sweet scent and delicate flowers of the sweet pea. Seeds are sown outdoors in spring and the plants present little or no problem when it comes to cultivation. Their pink, white, cream, pale yellow, blue, mauve, purple and crimson flowers can be enjoyed the summer through, and many varieties have bicoloured blooms. There are numerous excellent named strains offered by seedsmen. The plants climb by means of tendrils and, though the purists would have you remove these to ensure larger flowers, their presence makes tying in unnecessary. A height of 2 m (6 ft) is normal, though plants trained on single stems may make 3 m (10 ft).

If you want something more permanent than *Lathyrus odoratus*, the annual sweet pea, then grow *L. latifolius*, the everlasting pea. This is a hardy perennial climber with deep pink, pale pink or white blooms held on stiff stems from mid- to late summer. It grows 2.5 m (8 ft) tall.

POSITION AND SOIL

Both plants enjoy a position against a warm fence or wall, or an open sunny spot where they can be trained over tree stumps or arches, or else up a tripod of bamboo canes or bean poles. The soil should not dry out too quickly in sunny weather and it needs to be enriched with good helpings of well-rotted manure or compost before sowing or planting.

CULTIVATION

Plant the everlasting pea in spring or autumn and mulch the soil around established specimens with manure or compost every spring. Through the summer feed both types of pea fortnightly with diluted liquid fertilizer. Remove faded flowerheads to prolong the flowering season and water the plants well in dry, sunny weather.

PRUNING AND TRAINING

The everlasting pea should be cut back to ground level in autumn. The annual sweet pea only lasts a season and will be killed by the onset of frosts. Both types of plant need wires or wire netting to cling to if planted against the flat surface of a fence or wall. Up bamboo canes, bean poles or brushwood branches pushed into the ground they will grow happily, though preliminary ties are necessary to show them the way. Exhibitors grow sweet peas in rows, training each plant up its own string, pinching out tendrils, disbudding, tying in and what have you.

PROPAGATION

Seeds of the sweet pea are sown outdoors at the foot of the supports on which the plants are to flower in early and mid-spring, or in peat pots in a warm greenhouse in late winter for planting out in mid-spring. The seeds have a very thick coat and may germinate more readily if 'nicked' on one side with a penknife. The everlasting pea can be propagated by dividing mature plants in autumn (the transplants may take some time to settle down and flower well), or seed can be sown in pots placed in a cold frame or cool greenhouse in spring or early summer.

LIPPIA

Lippia citriodora, the lemon-scented verbena, has become very popular in the past few years. It has always been grown by herbalists for the strong lemon fragrance of its long, pointed leaves, and now gardeners seem to have discovered that it is a delightful plant to grow against a warm wall where it can be protected from the severe winters it dislikes. It is deciduous and can reach a height of 3 m (10 ft) or so, though 1.25–2 m (4–6 ft) is more common. The flowers are pale lilac in colour but so small as to be invisible from a distance. Do try this plant, if only to produce headily scented leaves for use in home-made pot-pourris.

POSITION AND SOIL
A south- or west-facing wall will give lippia the protection it needs, and it prefers a light, well-drained soil.

CULTIVATION
Plant in spring. Container-grown specimens transplant best. Mulch the soil around the plant with well-rotted garden compost each spring. Bracken or straw laid around and among the branches of the shrub in winter will afford it extra protection.

PRUNING AND TRAINING
All dead and frost-damaged stems should be cut back in spring to buds that are breaking into growth. As the plants grow taller their stems can be tied to horizontal wires held against the wall with vine eyes.

PROPAGATION
Cuttings of firm young growths can be rooted in a propagating frame in summer.

LONICERA

No country cottage garden would be complete without its fragrant honeysuckle sprawling over a rustic arch or gateway. *Lonicera periclymenum* is the commonest species, also known as woodbine, and I think it is one of the best. Each flower is composed of many florets, at first finger-like and then opening like dragons' mouths and turning from crimson in the bud to pale yellow. The sweet scent is pleasantly overpowering. The plant will reach a height of 6 m (20 ft) on a suitable support and has two good varieties: 'Belgica', the early Dutch honeysuckle flowering in late spring, early summer and again in early autumn; and 'Serotina' the late Dutch honeysuckle which flowers from mid-summer to early autumn.

There are many more species but I really have room to mention only two of them: *L. japonica aureoreticulata*, a semi-evergreen shrub with long, questing stems whose small green leaves are veined with bright yellow, and *L. sempervirens*, the trumpet honeysuckle, an evergreen with orange and yellow flowers (with no fragrance) and round leaves, many of which are pierced by the stems. Both can reach 10 m (30 ft).

POSITION AND SOIL

All the honeysuckles like sun, but the evergreen *L. sempervirens* and *L. japonica aureoreticulata* will tolerate some shade. The first of these two is a little tender and best grown against a wall where it is sheltered from winds. *L. periclymenum* and its varieties can be grown over arches, pergolas, tree stumps and up walls. Generally speaking they are like clematis in that they like a cool root run and their heads in the sun. Ordinary soil, enriched with a little well-rotted compost or manure at planting time, will suit them fine.

CULTIVATION

Plant deciduous honeysuckles in autumn, evergreen kinds in autumn or spring. Container-grown specimens transplant best.

PRUNING AND TRAINING

'The fragrant honeysuckle clambers clockwise to the sun', sang Messrs Flanders and Swann, reminding us that the plant is a twiner. Provide it with the support of your choice (fixing wires or trellis against the flat surface of fences or walls), tie in the first shoots and the plant will do the rest. Prune *L. sempervirens* and *L. periclymenum* and its varieties immediately after flowering, cutting out several of the older stems that have carried flowers. This annual thinning should keep the plants in good shape. *L. japonica aureoreticulata* can be clipped back each spring to restrict and renew its growth. Individual stems can be chopped from any of the plants if they are making a nuisance of themselves through the summer.

PROPAGATION

Cuttings of firm young growths can be rooted in a propagating frame in summer; suitably pendant stems can be layered in spring or autumn.

MAGNOLIA

Large, glossy evergreen leaves and, in summer and autumn, elegant, scented, cup-shaped blooms with thick creamy petals make *Magnolia grandiflora* the most stately of wall plants. It needs a large sheltered wall where it can stretch itself in the sun, and even when not in flower it is good to look at because its shiny green leaves have rusty undersides. Usually the laurel magnolia or bull bay, as it is called, grows to about 14 m (40 ft). There are several varieties with leaves and flowers of slightly different shapes and sizes.

POSITION AND SOIL

A south- or west-facing wall is necessary and the plant grows best in the south and west parts of the country. Enrich the soil with well-rotted compost or manure at planting time. This species is one of the few magnolias which will tolerate chalky soil.

CULTIVATION
Plant in spring. Container-grown specimens transplant best. Mulch the soil around the plant with manure, compost or leaf-mould each spring.

PRUNING AND TRAINING
Very little, if any, pruning is needed. Only branches which are out-growing their allotted space should be pruned out in spring. The main stem of a young plant should be tied in to horizontal wires fixed to the wall with vine eyes, and other stems should be tied in as they grow.

PROPAGATION
Layer suitably pendant branches in spring.

PARTHENOCISSUS

One of the 'big three' creepers (the other two being vitis and ampelopsis), this is the name under which the Virginia creeper is to be found. *Parthenocissus quinquefolia* is its full tongue-twisting title and its habit is equally convoluted. The green, much-divided vine-like leaves emerge in spring and turn scarlet and crimson in autumn before they fall. The plant reached the top of our two-storey house wall in two summers but it does need wires to support its stems which, although furnished with tendrils, are not entirely self-sufficient. *P. tricuspidata*, the Boston ivy, is entirely self-supporting and will cling like a leech to the surface of a fence or wall. The variety 'Veitchii' has smaller leaves, and on both plants they are glossy and richly coloured in autumn. *P. henryana* is the most sophisticated species, for its leaves are deeply cut and a shade of bronzy-plum veined with grey green. It is self-supporting and again the leaves burnish beautifully with the arrival of the cold weather. All these species carry blue-black fruits in good summers. It does not seem necessary to estimate their height. You provide the object and they'll cover it.

POSITION AND SOIL
These plants tolerate walls of any aspect, although they usually colour up better in autumn if they get some sun. They can be grown up old trees or buildings and quickly take them over. Ordinary well-drained soil is all they need.

CULTIVATION
Plant in autumn. Container-grown specimens transplant best.

PRUNING AND TRAINING
Prune in winter, removing all stems which have outgrown the space available, and cutting back all lateral branches to within two or three buds of a main stem. Keep the stems away from windows, gutters and

roofs or they will cause damage. Do not plant them against walls covered with pebbledash. *P. quinquefolia* needs horizontal wires to cling to if the surface is smooth. Space out the stems as they extend. The two other species need no encouragement for they will cling with their adhesive trendrils.

PROPAGATION

Cuttings of firm young growths can be rooted in a propagating frame in summer; suitably pendent stems can be layered in spring or autumn.

Through old apple trees, over sheds and up walls, the golden-leafed hop imparts summer brilliance to its support system.

PASSIFLORA

The passion flower is a Brazilian native that is surprisingly hardy in sheltered gardens. *Passiflora caerulea* is the species most easily grown outdoors and its fingered evergreen leaves show off to perfection the complicated blue and white flowers. The common name for this plant comes from the said allusion of the various parts of the flower to the passion of Christ. The five petals and five sepals represent the apostles (minus Judas and either Peter or Doubting Thomas depending on your opinions!), the frill of blue filaments represents the crown of thorns, five anthers represent the wounds, three stigmas the nails, the hand-shaped leaves the hands of His persecutors and the tendrils the whip with which He was scourged.

From early to late summer the plant will bloom with abandon, and at the same time its tendril-clad stems will spread themselves over more territory. 'Constance Elliott' is a very reliable variety with large white flowers and, like the straight species, will reach a height of 6–10 m (20–30 ft) with ease. Orange, egg-shaped fruits are produced in good summers. They are edible but seedy.

POSITION AND SOIL
South- or west-facing walls are the best places for this plant. Ordinary soil is preferred; on rich ground the plants are all leaf and no flowers.

CULTIVATION
Plant in spring from containers. Leaf-mould can be worked into the soil at planting time. Protect the base of the plant with straw or bracken in winter in case it should be cut back by frost.

PRUNING AND TRAINING
Trellis or wire supports should be provided against walls and fences and the young stems can be spaced out and introduced to these in the first year. They will soon romp away, climbing by means of their tendrils. Flowers are carried on long, pendulous growths produced during the summer. Cut these back to within 8 or 10 cm (3 or 4 in) of the main stems in the spring following flowering. New shoots to carry the next summer's flowers will be produced from the dormant buds.

PROPAGATION
Cuttings of strong shoot tips can be rooted in a propagating frame in summer.

PHYGELIUS

Not strictly a climber, but a pretty flowering shrub which will grow well in a warm and sheltered spot by a wall, is *Phygelius capensis*, the

Cape figwort. Large, open heads of tubular red flowers are thrust above the dark evergeeen leaves in late summer and they last for several weeks. Much of the growth is cut back by frost in winter but the plant will usually survive and shoots will be pushed out lower down on the stem the following spring. In the open phygelius normally grows 60–100 cm (2–3 ft) high, but when the stems are tied in to a warm wall it can reach 2 m (6 ft) or more.

POSITION AND SOIL
A south- or west-facing wall and ordinary well-drained soil will produce good plants.

CULTIVATION
Plant out in the spring. Container-grown specimens transplant best.

PRUNING AND TRAINING
Tie in a framework of sturdy branches to horizontal wires held against the wall with vine eyes, or grow the plant as a free-standing shrub if you prefer. Cut back all frost-damaged growths to healthy green shoots in spring.

PROPAGATION
Seeds can be sown in a warm greenhouse in spring; cuttings of firm young growths can be rooted in a propagating frame in summer; suckers can be removed with a portion of the root system and transplanted in spring.

PIPTANTHUS

Known as the evergreen laburnum because of the similarity of its leaves to that plant, *Piptanthus laburnifolius* is a strong-growing shrub well suited to wall culture by virtue of its habit and its tenderness. Although they will remain on the plant in mild winters, the evergreen leaves are shed if cold weather really takes a hold. Three oval, pointed leaflets are carried on each stalk, and clusters of yellow pea-like flowers appear in front of them in late spring. The plant will grow quickly to 3 m (10 ft) or so, but in spite of its vigour has a tendency to be rather short lived in some gardens. Not to worry – it is good while it lasts and easily propagated.

POSITION AND SOIL
Give piptanthus the protection of a sunny south- or west-facing wall and grow it in ordinary well-drained soil. It does not like chalk.

CULTIVATION
Plant in spring. Container-grown specimens transplant best.

PRUNING AND TRAINING
Piptanthus is a wall shrub which looks best if it is not tied in, although

The rich blue flowers of the morning glory are an irresistible invitation to sit out on a sunny patio.

the main stems may be anchored loosely to the wall for stability. Pruning consists of removing one or two older branches each spring, cutting them out at ground level and allowing strong young growths thrown up from the base of the plant to replace them. Any frost-damaged shoots should also be cut out in spring.

PROPAGATION
Seeds can be sown in pots placed in a garden frame in spring: cuttings of firm young growths can be rooted in a propagating frame in summer or early autumn.

POLYGONUM

For the desperate gardener, anxious and impatient to find something that will cover an eyesore or make a green screen, *Polygonum baldschuanicum* is the answer to his prayer. Its common names are Russian vine and mile-a-minute, both of which aptly sum up its characteristics. The advantages of the plant are its rate of growth (up to 5 m (15 ft), in a season), the fact that it makes a dense screen of twining shoots and deciduous green leaves, and its display of frothy white flowers which appear in mid-summer and continue into autumn. It is an exceptionally accommodating plant but rather dull when out of flower; still, its advantages may well outweigh this demerit in your particular situation.

POSITION AND SOIL
The Russian vine likes sun, but will also perform well in shade, and it will grow in any soil. When trained against fences or walls it should be provided with trellis or wire supports, but through old trees, over tree stumps, arches and pergolas its twining stems can usually get a grip on their own. Dilapidated garden sheds and garages can be masked (and supported!) by this climber if they are first equipped with wires to support the stems. Avoid planting it alongside other garden buildings though for its stems will soon find a way inside and may lift the roof!

PRUNING AND TRAINING
Pruning is needed only when the plant outgrows its allotted space, and then it can be cut back in early spring before growth starts. As long as there is something for it to cling to it needs no help from the gardener.

PROPAGATION
Cuttings of firm young side-shoots (taken with a heel) can be rooted in a propagating frame in summer; hardwood cuttings can be inserted outdoors in autumn.

PYRACANTHA

The firethorns are among the hardiest of our evergreen garden shrubs which can be relied on to perform well in gardens throughout the country. Their stout stems, equipped with tough thorns and equally tough dark green leaves, carry clusters of creamy-white flowers in early summer followed by vast displays of orange, red or yellow berries in autumn and winter. Trained against walls or fences the firethorns will grow between 2.5 and 5 m (8 and 15 ft) high. Among the best species and varieties are: *Pyracantha atalantioides*, scarlet fruits; *P. coccinea* 'Lalandei', orange fruits, and *P. rogersiana* 'Flava', yellow fruits.

POSITION AND SOIL
North-, south-, east-, and west-facing walls or fences are all suitable, and any soil will be tolerated.

CULTIVATION
Plant in spring or autumn from containers. Young plants seem to establish themselves more quickly than mature specimens. The maturing berries can be disfigured by a brown scab disease similar to that which attacks apples. Spray at petal fall with mancozeb as a preventive measure.

PRUNING AND TRAINING
Cut back after flowering those stems which are outgrowing the space available. Other than this no pruning is necessary and flowering will suffer if the shrub is trimmed too hard. Tie in the main stems to wires attached to fences and walls with vine eyes. Space out the main stems fan-wise in the first few years.

PROPAGATION
Cuttings of firm young growths can be rooted in a propagating frame in summer.

ROSA

No garden is complete without at least a handful of roses. Rich colours, variety of form and exquisite perfumes are to be found in abundance in this favourite group of plants. It is the climbers and ramblers that are suited to wall, fence, arch, pillar and pergola culture, and of these there are several distinct types. Some of them have been propagated from 'sports' (freak climbing stems sent out by ordinary hybrid tea or floribunda roses), some of them are repeat-flowering and others have just one glorious flush of bloom and a rambling rather than a climbing habit. A good rose book will give you the detailed background to all these groups; I shall have to content myself with recommending a list of tried and tested varieties followed by details on cultivation and pruning. The number given after each variety refers to the way in which it is best pruned (for details see under pruning and training, pp. 66–7).

TWENTY OF THE BEST

'Alberic Barbier'	Yellow in bud, creamy white when open; double; fragrant; summer-flowering rambler; vigorous (3)
'Albertine'	Deep salmon in bud, paler pink when open; double; fragrant; summer-flowering rambler; vigorous (3)

'Aloha'	Deep rose pink tinged with orange when young; double; fragrant; repeat-flowering climber; moderately vigorous (1)
'American Pillar'	Cerise pink with white eye; single; no fragrance; summer-flowering rambler; vigorous (3)
'Casino'	Clear yellow; double; no fragrance; repeat flowering climber; vigorous (4)
'Climbing Cecile Brunner'	Small blush-pink blooms; double; fragrant; summer-flowering climber; vigorous (3)
'Compassion'	Salmon-shaded orange; double; fragrant; repeat-flowering climber; vigorous (4)
'Danse du Feu'	Orange-red; semi-double; no fragrance; repeat-flowering climber; vigorous (1)
'Dorothy Perkins'	Rose pink; double; no fragrance; summer-flowering rambler; vigorous (2)
'Gloire de Dijon'	Buff yellow tinged pink; double; fragrant; repeat-flowering climber; vigorous (4)
'Golden Showers'	Bright yellow, fading with age; semi-double; fragrant; repeat-flowering climber; moderately vigorous (1)
'Handel'	Creamy white edged bright pink; double; no fragrance; repeat-flowering climber; vigorous (1)
'Climbing Iceberg'	White; double; no fragrance; summer-flowering climber; vigorous (4)
'Kiftsgate'	Creamy white flowers in large clusters; single; fragrant; summer flowering; (form of *R. filipes*); extremely vigorous, for large gardens only (1)
'Mermaid'	Soft yellow with orange stamens; single; no fragrance; repeat-flowering climber; vigorous (1)
'New Dawn'	Flesh pink; double; fragrant; repeat-flowering rambler; moderately vigorous (3)
'Parkdirektor Riggers'	Rich crimson; semi-double; no fragrance; repeat-flowering climber; vigorous (4)
'Paul's Scarlet'	Scarlet; semi-double; no fragrance; summer-flowering rambler; vigorous (3)
'Pink Perpetue'	Light pink with darker shading; double; no fragrance; repeat-flowering climber; vigorous (4)
'Zephirine Drouhin'	Carmine pink; semi-double; fragrant; thornless; repeat-flowering climber; vigorous (1)

POSITION AND SOIL

A sunny spot is preferred by all roses, though there are one or two which can be grown on north-facing walls ('Mermaid' is a good example). Arches, pergolas, colonnades, trellis screens, walls and fences all make suitable supports, and vigorous specimens, e.g. *Rosa filipes* 'Kiftsgate', are seen to best advantage when allowed to grow through an old tree.

Any ordinary garden soil is suitable provided that it is not likely to dry out in summer. The soil should be well dug and enriched with plenty of well-rotted manure or garden compost plus a good sprinkling of bonemeal before planting.

CULTIVATION

Plant in autumn, or at any time of the year if container-grown plants are purchased (but pay good attention to watering in the first few months). Do not plant nearer than 45 cm (18 in) from a wall or the trunk of a tree. Mulch annually in spring with manure or compost, applying a dusting of rose fertilizer at the same time, and again a month or so later. Keep a look-out for blackspot and mildew (spraying with benomyl or one of the modern 'cocktail' rose sprays that control both fungi and insects if they are seen), and for greenfly (aphids), which can be controlled by spraying with pirimicarb.

PRUNING AND TRAINING

Pruning methods differ for climbing and rambling roses depending on their vigour and on the type of wood which produces the flowers. In the list of varieties each plant is given a number which indicates the method of pruning which suits it. These methods are as follows:

1) Remove only dead, weak and very old exhausted stems, between midwinter and early spring.
2) Cut out at ground level all stems which have carried flowers and tie in new stems to replace them. Prune these varieties in late summer and early autumn.
3) Retain all new stems (some may arise from quite high up on the older branches) and cut out older wood where possible, removing at least one old branch each year. Prune these varieties in late summer and early autumn.
4) Remove stems only when they overcrowd the main framework. Cut out dead and diseased wood and shorten the laterals (the smaller shoots coming from the main stem) to three buds. Prune these varieties between midwinter and early spring. Do *not* prune roses in this group during the first year after planting. Some of them are climbing sports of hybrid tea and floribunda roses which will revert and become bushy if pruned too early.

Roses other than those in group 4 can be cut back to a height of 15 cm (6 in) or so immediately after planting to encourage the formation of a

Even the most unskilled gardener can produce flowers on the winter jasmine at a time when the rest of the garden looks bleak and bare.

good framework of stems. However, they can be left unpruned if you prefer, and the extension growths of the first season tied in and used as the basic framework.

Whatever support system is used the stems of the roses will have to be tied in. On pergolas, arches and pillars the stems can be gently wound round the support and tied into position. On colonnades they are taken up the posts and then along the ropes. On walls, fences and screens the main framework of stems should be spread out fan-wise and tied to trellis-work or horizontal wires. Roses which are to be trained through trees can be shown the way with a stout cane or stake angled into the branches. Once into the crown of the tree they will find their own way about.

PROPAGATION
Hardwood cuttings can be inserted outdoors in early and mid-autumn; suitably pendent stems can be layered in autumn.

SCHIZOPHRAGMA

Don't let this plant's ugly name put you off growing it, for it is extremely useful against a shady wall or fence. Two species are in general cultivation; *Schizophragma hydrangeoides* and *S. integrifolium*. The latter is rather larger in leaf and flower than the former but both are of a similar appearance. The deciduous leaves are like those of the climbing hydrangea and the creamy white flowers produced from midsummer to autumn are similar too, but the plants are generally more showy than their distant relation.

Both species are very vigorous, eventually reaching a height of 10 m (30 ft), and they climb by means of aerial roots in a similar fashion to ivy. *S. hydrangeoides* has a pretty pale pink-flowered form called 'Roseum'.

POSITION AND SOIL
Though a shady spot suits them well, schizophragmas will flower best of all on a sunny wall, proving that they can be grown successfully in a variety of situations. They are particularly happy running over tree stumps and through trees where they can be left to their own devices. Any ordinary soil will content them, though it is a good idea to enrich it with well-rotted manure or compost at planting time.

CULTIVATION
Plant in autumn. Container-grown specimens transplant best. Mulch the soil around the plant with manure or compost each spring for the first few years after planting.

PRUNING AND TRAINING
Though it will cling well on its own, a few wires fixed to the wall will give schizophragma a little extra support. Only the main stems need be tied in. Prune out in winter only those stems which are not required to extend the plant and any which are weak or dead.

PROPAGATION
Cuttings of firm young growths can be rooted in a propagating frame in summer; suitably pendent shoots can be layered in spring or autumn.

SENECIO

I want to mention only one senecio but to do that I must mention three. Most people know it as *Senecio greyi*, we are told that it is really *S. laxifolius*, botanists have suggested that it is a cross between the two and it has recently been christened *S.* 'Sunshine'. If I haven't lost you already let me say that your local nursery or garden centre will most probably have this superb grey-leaved evergreen shrub which is covered with bright yellow daisy flowers in summer, and whatever they call it you should give it a try. It does not climb but will form a 2 m (6 ft) wide mound of rounded leaves at the base of a sunny wall or fence, even in the most inhospitable soil.

Adventurous gardeners who like the unusual can try tying some of its stems to horizontal wires fixed to the wall, for it can be trained upwards quite effectively in such a fashion, its sideshoots cascading gently downwards.

POSITION AND SOIL

A south-facing wall or fence will give this plant what it likes – a sunny spot in which to bask – and light, well-drained, even dry soil suits it best. However, it can be grown successfully on clay and it thrives in coastal districts.

CULTIVATION

Plant in spring or autumn. This plant is hardier than is sometimes suggested.

PRUNING AND TRAINING

Thin out the shrub by cutting back about half its shoots each spring, removing them almost flush with the main stem. This will encourage the production of new shoots and will keep the bush dense rather than straggly. Longer, woody branches can be cut out at the same time if the shrub is an old one that has got out of hand. Tying in to wires held against the wall with vine eyes is necessary if you want to train the plant flat against the wall.

PROPAGATION

Cuttings of firm young growths can be rooted in a propagating frame in summer.

SOLANUM

Imagine the flowers of a tomato grouped together in clusters of thirty or more and only the centre of each bloom remaining yellow, the petals being rich lilac purple. Scatter these flowers over scrambling stems 6 m (25 ft) long and you have the delectable S. crispum, a slightly tender climber for a sunny wall.

I am full of admiration for this plant because it strikes me as being so versatile. You can grow it on its own very successfully (as a scrambler or as a free-standing shrub), but plant it where it can venture through a neighbouring climber and you can enjoy it in company. It is particularly at home with Abutilon vitifolium for the flowering seasons of the two plants neatly overlap – the abutilon flowers from late spring to midsummer and the solanum from early summer to early autumn.

The variety of *S. crispum* known as 'Glasnevin' is reputedly hardier than the straight species and will usually flower until mid-autumn.

Solanum jasminoides is the only other species worth cultivating outdoors, though it is more tender still than *S. crispum*. It is vigorous, reaching 8 m (25 ft) or more and bears pale blue flowers with yellow centres from midsummer until the frosts of autumn. There is a white form called 'Album'.

POSITION AND SOIL

A sunny, sheltered wall is essential for *S. jasminoides*, and a light, well-drained soil is preferable. *S. crispum* will tolerate chalk and in sheltered gardens can be trained over sheds, garages and summerhouses and through old trees.

CULTIVATION

Plant in spring. Container-grown specimens will establish themselves best.

PRUNING AND TRAINING

Tie in the stems to wires or trellis-work attached to the wall, spreading them out fan-wise in the first few years to give even coverage. Prune in spring, cutting all weak side-shoots back to strong buds and removing frost-burned growths. When grown through another shrub the stems can be loosely tied in to the branches of their host.

PROPAGATION

Cuttings of firm young growths can be rooted in a propagating frame in summer.

THUNBERGIA

Black-eyed Susan, or *Thunbergia alata*, to give its proper name, is an attractive climber whose wide-faced orange, yellow or white flowers are centred with a blackish-purple blotch. Though it will survive in a warm spot outdoors only until the frosts of autumn it makes up for its short stay by producing lots of growth and lots of flowers. It will reach a height of about 2 m (6 ft), or maybe a little less, and its green leaves make a good backcloth for the bright flowers.

POSITION AND SOIL

A warm, sunny wall or fence and a patch of fertile soil will grow good plants. Alternatively they can be planted in large pots or tubs (John Innes No. 2 potting compost is suitable) and trained up tripods of bamboo canes. On warm patios and roof gardens they will do well in these containers.

CULTIVATION

Plant out pot-grown plants in late spring when danger of frost is past.

Water the soil well in dry spells.

PRUNING AND TRAINING

No pruning is necessary for although this is a perennial climber it is grown as an annual outdoors and can be pulled up when killed off by autumn frosts. Tie in the young shoots to wires or trellis-work attached to a wall or fence, or else to tripods of canes in containers. Once they have a grip they will romp away happily.

PROPAGATION

Sow seeds in a warm greenhouse in spring. Pot up the seedlings individually and grow on until planting time, gradually hardening them off.

If the birds always pinch the berries off your red firethorn, try a yellow-fruited variety such as *Pyracantha rogersiana* 'Flava'.

TROPAEOLUM

The good old nasturtium, *Tropaeolum majus*, is one of the first plants that budding gardeners encounter at a very early age. There are bushy and trailing varieties, but also those which climb vigorously, decorating walls, bamboo tripods and tall stems of brushwood with their parasol-like leaves and orange, yellow and red trumpets. In a good summer they will flower profusely and reach a height of 2 m (6 ft).

If you fancy something a little out of the ordinary try the Canary creeper, *T. peregrinum*, which has hand-shaped leaves and bright yellow frilly-petalled flowers that stare out from the foliage like tiny dragons. Both these varieties are annuals, which can be raised afresh from seed each year.

Tropaeolum speciosum is the Scotch flame flower, a perennial always seen at its best in Scottish gardens where it rambles through trees to a height of 3 m (10 ft) or more. It is a little difficult to settle in but once its fleshy roots are established it does not look back. Masses of small, bright red trumpets are produced in summer and autumn.

POSITION AND SOIL

The two annuals like a sunny spot in the open (where they can be grown up canes or clumps of twiggy branches), or against a warm wall or fence, and a light, rather poor soil. They are good in containers too where they can be trained up tripods of bamboo canes. The Scotch flame flower, on the other hand, prefers a shady aspect and a moist soil enriched with leaf-mould and peat. It dislikes dryness at the roots. Plant it on the north side of a tree (evergreens are particularly suitable) or on a north- or east-facing wall.

CULTIVATION

Plant the two annuals in late spring when danger of frost is past. Roots of *T. speciosum* should be planted horizontally 8 cm (3 in) deep in spring at the foot of the plant's intended support.

PRUNING AND TRAINING

Pruning is not necessary. All three species are cut to the ground by frost in autumn – the perennial one will grow again in spring, the other two will not. Once introduced to their supports the stems will twine and hold on with no further assistance.

PROPAGATION

Both the annual species can be raised from seeds sown individually in peat pots in a cool greenhouse in spring; *T. majus* can be sown outdoors where it is to grow in late spring. Seeds of *T. speciosum* can be sown in pots in a cold frame in spring; roots can be divided in spring but new plants may take some time to establish themselves.

VITIS

The vines not included under ampelopsis and parthenocissus are to be found here. For reasons of space I shall stick to just two, both of which are superbly decorative and well worth a place in the garden. *Vitis* 'Brant' (or *V. vinifera* 'Brandt') is a vigorous climber whose vine leaves take on brilliant tints in autumn before they fall. Its greatest attribute, however, is that it carries small blue-black grapes which ripen to perfection in a good summer and are delicious to eat. In a warm spot the plant will reach as much as 6 m (20 ft) high, and more if given the room to grow.

Of all the vines the boldest and most stately is undoubtedly *V. coignetiae*. Its rough but downy elephantine leaves are held out boldly from scrambling stems and before they are shed in autumn they turn the most breathtaking shades of orange, mahogany, crimson and scarlet. The sight of the mid-autumn sun on this plant will not be forgotten. Blackish-purple fruits are produced but are of minor value compared with the leaves. The plant is extremely vigorous.

POSITION AND SOIL

A sunny spot produces the best autumn colour (and the best fruits) and a fertile soil the strongest plants. These vines will grow on walls, fences, buildings, pergolas and arches and also through old fruit trees or over large tree-stumps.

CULTIVATION

Plant in autumn, working a generous helping of well-rotted manure or garden compost into the ground. The same material can be given as a mulch each spring.

PRUNING AND TRAINING

Where space is not a problem the vines can be left to grow unrestricted. However, in most small gardens their growth needs to be controlled. During the first few years tie in the main branches to make a well-spaced framework. Cut back the side-shoots in early winter so that only three buds are left on each. If pruned much later than this the cut surfaces may bleed, an indication that the sap is rising. Tie in the shoots to be retained, either to wires or trellis on a wall or fence, or to the uprights and horizontal bars on arches and pergolas, or to the trunk and lower branches of trees. Once established the stems can cling quite well, though wayward ones may need a little encouragement from time to time.

PROPAGATION

Suitably pendent shoots can be layered in spring or autumn; cuttings of firm young growths can be rooted in a propagating frame in summer.

WISTERIA

If I had to pick just one climber out of the whole list I think it would be wisteria. In our last house I used to write in an upstairs bedroom, and on a late spring evening, hundreds of long lilac-purple flower trails would hang outside my window scenting the air with their intoxicating fragrance. The species trained around the house was *Wisteria sinensis*, the Chinese wisteria. It is certainly the commonest kind in cultivation but also one of the very best. As the flowers fade the rich green pinnate leaves will emerge to clothe the brickwork in a thick coat of foliage, and the twining stems will extend the plant's territory at the rate of 2 m (6 ft) or more a year. A lighter flush of flowers is often produced in early autumn. This species will grow to 15 m (50 ft) in height depending on the means of support.

Wisteria floribunda is the next most popular species, and its form 'Macrobotrys' has the most spectacular flower trails – often 60–100 cm (2–3 ft) long. It is not so vigorous as *W. sinensis* for it grows to only 5 m (15 ft) or so.

The plant was named after Professor Caspar Wistar of Pennsylvania and is often called wistaria, but due to the odd laws of nomenclature we must really call it wisteria for that is how it was mistakenly registered.

POSITION AND SOIL

Wisterias do like sun, so plant on a south- or west-facing wall, or else in a sunny spot at the foot of an arch, pergola or old tree. Always ensure that you buy a grafted plant which will be of proven flowering quality. Cutting-raised plants are sometimes shy of blooming. The plants look particularly attractive, and essentially oriental, when trained over bridges where their reflection can be enjoyed in the water. A good, fertile soil is preferred (work in plenty of well-rotted compost or manure at planting time) and although wisterias will tolerate chalk, the addition of some good soil and leaf-mould will produce better plants.

CULTIVATION

Plant in spring from containers. Mulch with well-rotted leaf-mould in spring and apply two or three liquid feeds of diluted tomato fertilizer through the summer (two or three gallons at a time). This treatment seems to persuade the plant to flower regularly. Sparrows and late frosts are both damaging to flower buds and both are difficult to deter. Content yourself in the knowledge that the frosts occur relatively infrequently and the birds are a nuisance in relatively few gardens. Where they are a real problem netting is the answer.

PRUNING AND TRAINING

In summer reduce the length of all the new growths not required to

It may only flower in one huge flush, but the spectacle of the rambling rose 'Albertine' in full bloom is unforgettable.

extend the plant. Cut them back to leave five or six leaves. In midwinter all side-shoots can be shortened to three buds. This pruning encourages the formation of flower buds. On walls horizontal wires should be held in place with vine eyes and the wisteria stems to be retained are spaced out and tied in to these supports as they grow. On pergolas, arches and bridges the new stems should be fastened to the framework with stout twine and the woody old ones with loosely looped wire. Cut out old wood only when it is dead. Mature branches age picturesquely and still carry plenty of flowers on their young side-shoots.

PROPAGATION

Cuttings of firm young growths can be rooted in a propagating frame in summer but only bother to take them from free-flowering plants; suitable shoots can be layered in spring or summer. Plants raised from seeds are often very slow to flower. If your wisteria still fails to bloom when you have followed these cultural recommendations for five years or so (wait a little longer for *W. floribunda*) you would be well advised to dig it up, enrich the soil and plant a specimen known to have been propagated from a free-flowering plant.

CHAPTER 4

SOIL PREPARATION

Most of the climbers and wall plants described in this book are perennial; that is, given the right conditions they will live for many years. For this reason it is vitally important to spend a little time on preparing the piece of ground they are to occupy, and to put into it all that the plants will need in the way of sustenance. Some plants are more greedy than others: annuals grow best in poor soils as a rule; more vigorous perennials like something to sink their teeth into.

GARDEN SOIL

One vital requirement of all plants is moisture. Like us they cannot survive without water, but they can also be killed by excessive amounts. The ideal soil (if such there be) is one which never becomes waterlogged, yet never dries to dust. Now if this sounds rather pie in the sky let me explain how your ordinary back garden soil can be made to fit the bill. If it is badly drained then you will have to make provisions for the water to be removed, either along slightly sloping trenches which are excavated, partly filled with rubble, and then refilled with soil, or by means of land drains or land tiles. These are pipes laid below the ground to fulfil the same purpose as rubble-filled trenches. Contractors will advise you more thoroughly on both methods.

However, if your soil is against a building or tree, drought rather than excessive moisture is likely to be the problem, and waterlogged soils are likely to be found in relatively few gardens. Backbreaking heavy clay and light blow-away sand can both be improved by the addition of 'organic matter'. This blanket term covers animal manures, garden compost, rotted leaves and any other plant or animal waste. The manure or compost will force the sticky particles of clay soil apart, so improving drainage, and will help sandy soils to hold more moisture than they would do otherwise.

But before the enrichment can be added the soil must be turned to let in air and to allow the removal of weeds. Use a well-made spade that is comfortable to hold and dig the ground thoroughly, turning over each spadeful of soil so that it is completely inverted. Persistent thick-rooted weeds should be pulled out and the annual ones turned in. The manure or compost can be incorporated as you dig at the rate of a couple of bucketsful to the square metre (yard). If you have the energy, take out a trench at one end of the bed or border, cart the soil to the other end of the plot and then start digging immediately behind the trench, throwing the soil forward into it. When you come to the end of the border throw the soil removed from the first trench into the last one. If you dig in this fashion the manure or compost can be thrown into the bottom of each trench where the plants' roots will soon find it, and the soil is more thoroughly cultivated.

The time of year at which you dig will depend on the time you intend to plant. For spring planting dig in autumn; for autumn planting dig in spring or summer.

About two weeks before planting, scatter two or three handfuls of blood, bone and fishmeal over each square metre (yard) of ground and lightly fork it in. This fertilizer is rich in nutrients which will encourage root activity.

Finally, remember to choose a plant that suits your soil, particularly if it contains chalk. The lists on pp. 13–17 will show you which plants enjoy particular soils and situations.

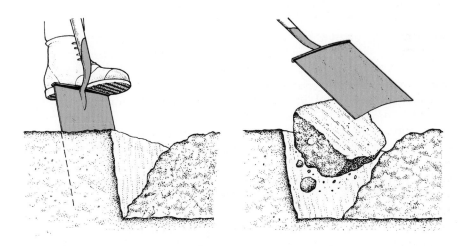

Fig. 6 Single or plain digging. Note that the ground is cultivated to the full depth of the spade

Fig. 7 Drainage holes in containers should be covered up with stones or pieces of broken flower pots to prevent their being clogged up with potting soil

SOIL IN CONTAINERS

Plants being grown in tubs or large pots have just the same requirements as those being grown in the open ground. However, they are more easily prepared for because potting composts such as John Innes No. 2 (for annuals) and John Innes No. 3 (for perennials) will provide all they need in the way of nourishment for the first few months, and they will hold water well. What the gardener must remember to do is check that the container has drainage holes to allow the escape of excess water (and to cover them with stones or broken flower pots to prevent them from becoming blocked), and that enough water is supplied to keep the soil moist, particularly in summer when it will dry out very rapidly.

CHAPTER 5

BUYING, PLANTING AND SUPPORTING

BUYING

If you want to choose from a wide range of healthy and properly named plants, do your shopping at a reputable nursery or garden centre. People who grow plants for a living are generally better acquainted with the likes and dislikes of their stock and will be able to provide you with reliable information on cultivation.

Do not go for the largest plant, but for the one with the best framework of branches. Small plants will often establish themselves more quickly than their larger relations and although not much to look at when planted will soon grow by leaps and bounds. Added to this they will also be cheaper.

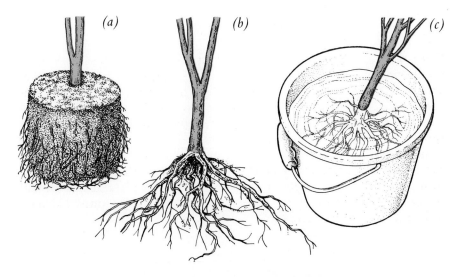

Fig. 8 (a) Container-grown plant with a well-developed root system in a good 'ball' of soil; (b) 'bare-root' plant which has been lifted from the open ground; (c) the roots of all 'bare-root' plants should be soaked in a bucket of water overnight before planting.

Nurseries and garden centres offer both container-grown plants (Fig. 8a), and those lifted from the open ground known as 'bare-root' plants (Fig. 8b). Plants grown in containers will have a well-developed root system in a good 'ball' of soil and can be planted, weather permitting, at any time of year. Bare-root plants are lifted from the nursery rows between late autumn and early spring and replanted as soon as possible afterwards. Container-grown plants can usually be collected from the nursery at any time on a cash-and-carry basis, but bare-root plants should be ordered well before the planting season to make sure of their availability. Planting times given in the A – Z section refer to bare-root plants, though reference is made to container-grown specimens where these are best planted at a particular time.

Certain chain stores offer climbing plants and other shrubs packed in

Fig. 9 (a) – (e) Planting a bare-root plant – see text for details. (f) Diagram showing the use of vine eyes to hold plant-supporting wires

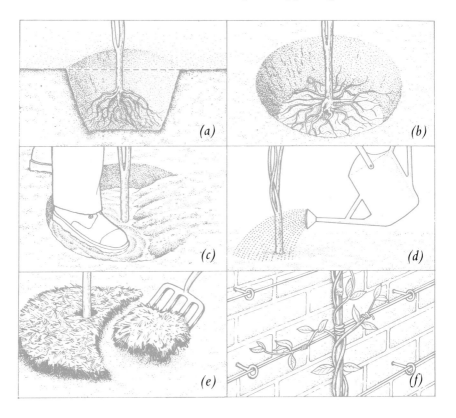

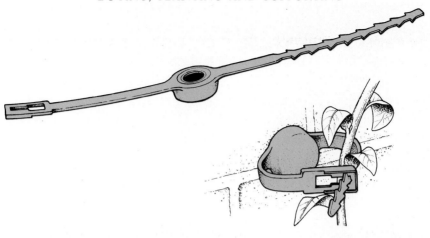

Fig. 10 A knob of epoxy resin, supplied with this plastic 'plant sticker', enables the device to be stuck securely to the wall.

polythene bags. If you must buy these do check that they are fresh in and have not been sitting on the counter for weeks. Many large specialist nurseries sell by mail order and most of these can be relied upon to despatch fresh plants properly packed. Before planting, strip away the packing and soak the roots of all bare-root shrubs in a bucket of water overnight to make sure that they are not dry.

PLANTING

Take your time and do the job properly. If the soil is too wet or frozen hard when the plants arrive, stand them in a sheltered corner (if they are pot-grown) or take out a hole or short trench in the garden, place the plant's roots in it and replace the soil. This is known as heeling in and the plants will be perfectly happy in this state for several weeks until conditions improve.

When the soil is nice and moist but not wet, planting can be carried out as follows (Fig. *9a* − *e*):

a) Excavate a hole which is more than wide enough to take the plant's roots and deep enough to allow the old soil mark on the stem to rest just below the surface.

b) Remove the pot of a container-grown plant and do *not* disturb the roots. With bare-root plants the roots should be spread out evenly. Cut off with a sharp pair of secateurs any that are damaged or broken.

c) Gradually replace the soil, firming it with your foot as you do so. Finally, tidy up the surface of the soil with a fork.
d) Unless the soil is really moist always water plants in. Two or three watering cans full of water should be applied to really soak the soil.
e) Spread a 5 – 8 cm (2 – 3 in) layer of moist peat, leaf-mould, pulverised bark, garden compost, manure or other organic matter over the soil around the plant to act as a mulch (a layer that will retain moisture and suppress weeds).

The soil next to walls and tree trunks is likely to become very dry so always plant your climbers at least 30 – 45 cm (12 – 18 in) away from them, leading the stems towards their supports on bamboo canes.

SUPPORTING

On walls, flat fences and buildings, plants that do not cling by adhesive tendrils or aerial roots need something to hold on to. Stout galvanized wire strained between metal 'eyes' with long stems (vine eyes) is a long-lasting solution (Fig. 9f). Run the wires horizontally every 25 cm (10 in) up the wall. Young plants should always be led to these final supports with a cane or two up which their stems are trained. Alternatively trellis-work treated with preservative (not creosote) can be attached to the wall and the stems led through it.

Small green plastic 'plant stickers' are now on the market (Fig. 10) and make convenient anchors for single stems. They are fitted with a knob of epoxy resin which is supplied with them and stick securely to the wall if held in place for a few seconds.

There is little more to say about tripods, pergolas, arches and colonnades for these have been covered in Chapter 1, but remember that whatever the supports, young plants will need assistance to scale them in the early stages – a few preliminary ties should see them on their way.

If it's a yellow-flowered climbing rose you're seeking, plump for 'Golden Showers', for it s repeat flowering.

CHAPTER 6

TRAINING, PRUNING AND AFTERCARE

TRAINING

Once properly planted a climber will soon begin to establish its root system and the shoots will start to grow. If left to their own devices the stems may grow to a great length, but what is really needed in the early stages is not height but a good framework of well-spaced branches. For this reason it is advisable to pinch out the shoot tips of a young plant during the first year of its life if it looks like turning into a tall and spindly specimen. This pinching will spur the side-shoots into growth and a fuller branch system will be built up (Fig. 11*a*).

After this initial encouragement climbers grown through trees can usually be left to do their own thing. Those grown on walls, fences.

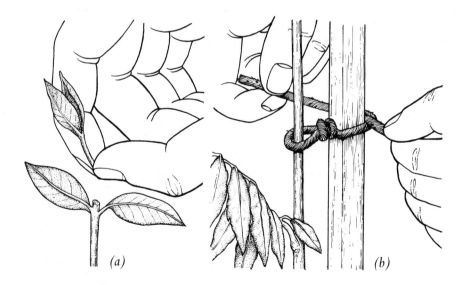

Fig. 11 (a) Pinching out the shoot tip of a young plant; (b) the stems of climbers should be loosely tied in to the support system with the use of strong garden twine

pergolas and other supports should be inspected every month or so and their stems loosely tied to the support with strong tarred twine (Fig. 11*b*). Heavier branches can be held in with slack wire loops. Space the stems evenly on the framework and avoid overcrowding.

Check your ties frequently through the year to make sure that they are secure but not strangling the stems they are supposed to be supporting.

PRUNING

Instructions on the timing of pruning and on the particular methods used are given for each plant in the A – Z list, but here I want to explain briefly why pruning is necessary and to give a few general tips.

Pruning is needed for three main reasons: (a) to control the size of a plant and to make it shapely; (b) to promote flowering; (c) to keep the plant healthy by removing dead, diseased and weak wood and encouraging new growth.

With certain plants pruning is not necessary. Rampant climbers

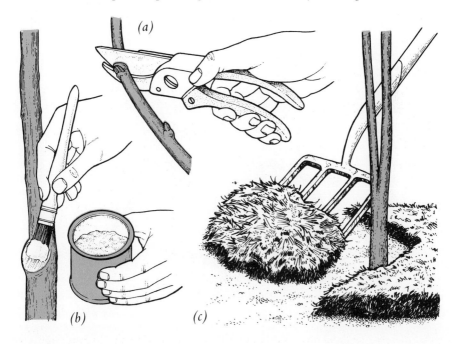

Fig. 12 (a) Pruning back to a bud with secateurs; (b) painting over large cut with bituminous wound dressing; (c) mulching

scrambling through trees usually grow well left on their own, and indeed pruning would be rather difficult to accomplish. Neither is pruning necessary on a regular basis with all shrubs; it is sufficient to cut back certain types only when they are in danger of outgrowing their allotted space and becoming a nuisance.

When you *do* prune use a sharp pair of secateurs or loppers and always cut back to a bud or else flush with the main stem (Fig. 12*a*). Never leave budless snags; these will only die back and they may allow diseases to enter. Paint large cuts over 2.5 cm (1 in) in diameter with a bituminous wound dressing to prevent the entry of disease (Fig. 12*b*).

Keep your eyes open for dead wood at all times and remove this as soon as it is seen. It is often more obvious in summer when the plants are in leaf.

AFTERCARE

It is good practice to mulch all permanent wall plants and climbers with a 5–8 cm (2–3 in) layer of moist organic matter each spring, and to replenish the layer when it shows signs of becoming thin. Apart from keeping the soil moist it will enrich it and suppress weeds. Coarse peat, well-rotted manure or garden compost, spent hops, spent mushroom compost and grass clippings can all be used, but make sure that the ground is moist before the mulch is applied (Fig. 12*c*).

The soil next to walls can quickly become bone dry in spring and summer, and sometimes in winter too. When it does, lay the hose-pipe

Fig. 13 Applying weedkiller to bare ground with watering can and dribble bar

on it for an hour or so to give it a thorough soaking. An odd canful of water will barely wet the surface and stands little chance of getting to the roots of mature plants and is therefore not very effective.

Two or three handfuls of a general fertilizer such as blood, bone and fish meal scattered over each square metre (yard) of soil around the plant will give it a welcome boost. Give the dressing twice – once in spring and again in early summer – and hoe it very lightly into the surface of the soil, disturbing the roots as little as possible.

If you grow annual and herbaceous plants around the base of your climbers I advise you to hand weed and mulch. If the ground is bare, or occupied by shrubs, then you can use a herbicide (weedkiller), but do allow the climber a year to establish itself first.

Before applying the herbicide clear the ground of any existing weeds by hand. On clean ground a residual weedkiller such as simazine can be used. Diluted in water and applied with a watering can and dribble-bar (Fig. 13) in early spring this chemical will keep the ground weed free for the summer, provided that the surface of the soil is left undisturbed.

CHAPTER 7

PROPAGATION

Few gardening jobs give more satisfaction than propagation. There is a certain delight in being able to take a packet of seeds or a few shoots and turn them into young plants with a life of their own. Not only is this operation great fun, but it also saves money; buy one plant and you can produce lots more from it at little extra cost.

All the plants mentioned in this book can be propagated from seeds or cuttings, by layering or division. For this reason I will not launch into a lengthy discourse on those two rather technical operations, budding and grafting.

SEEDS

All annual climbers, and a number of perennial ones, are easily raised from seeds. If you are collecting seeds from your own plants make sure that they are dry and fully ripe; do not pick a seedpod that is green and expect it to ripen indoors. Annuals are usually sown in pots and boxes in spring, either in a warm greenhouse or frame, or else on a windowsill where they will be warmed, but not scorched, by the sun.

A 10 cm (4 in) pot will normally hold more than enough seeds to produce a good supply of plants. Fill a plastic plant pot to its brim with moist John Innes seed compost, tamp this down with your fingers so that it is lightly firmed and then flatten the surface with the bottom of another plant pot. This should leave the compost about 1 cm (½ in) below the rim. Sow fine seeds thinly and cover them with compost shaken through a 0.5 cm (¼ in) sieve. As soon as the seeds disappear from view stop sieving, for they will then be sufficiently covered. Larger seeds can be pushed in with a pencil to one-and-a-half times their depth. Label the pot, water it using a can fitted with a fine rose, and then cover it with a piece of glass and a sheet of newspaper (Fig. 14) The dark, humid environment so created is ideal for germination. Stand the pot in your greenhouse or frame, or on a windowsill, and check it daily (turning the glass as you do so) to see if the seeds have germinated. When the first shoot breaks the surface remove the glass and paper. Water the compost gently if it shows signs of drying out.

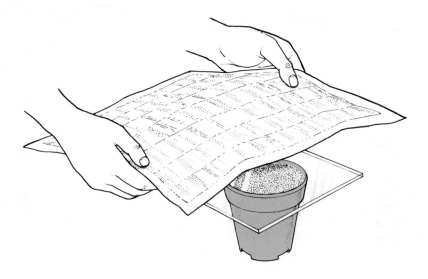

Fig. 14 Labelled pots of seeds should be covered with a piece of glass and a sheet of newspaper

Some seeds need cooler conditions and these can be sown in the same fashion but germinated out of doors without the glass and newspaper. A wooden or metal garden frame with a layer of gravel inside makes an ideal 'nursery' for these seeds.

As soon as the seedlings are large enough to handle they should be transplanted individually into 8 cm (3 in) pots of John Innes No. 1 potting compost or a peat-based equivalent. Handle the seedlings by their leaves and water them in.

All climbers grown from seed should be hardened off before being planted out. If raised indoors or in a greenhouse or frame they must be gradually given more ventilation to accustom them to outdoor temperatures.

Plant out annuals in late spring when danger of frost is past. Perennials can be potted on as necessary and planted out when they and the soil are ready.

CUTTINGS

There are three types of stem cuttings: softwood; half-ripe or semi-ripe, and hardwood.

The little yellow dragon flowers of *Tropaeolum peregrinum* sprout from the stems of this annual climber in summer.

Softwood cuttings are taken in early summer. Remove healthy shoot tips and prepare them by cutting below a leaf joint (or node) and removing the lowest leaves. You should end up with a soft shoot 5–8 cm (2–3 in) long, bare of leaves for two-thirds of its length. Dip the cut ends of the cuttings in rooting powder, tap off the excess, and dib them to half their depth around the edge of 10-cm (4-in) pots filled with a mixture of equal parts peat and sand (Fig. 15*b*).

Water the cuttings in and then place the pot in a propagating frame (a small version of the garden frame on the bench of a greenhouse) and cover the frame with polythene or a sheet of glass (Fig. 15*c*). If you do not possess this equipment the pot can easily be covered with a polythene bag held in place by an elastic band and stood on a windowsill out of direct sunlight.

As soon as they are rooted the cuttings will begin to grow and they can then be potted up in 8 cm (3 in) pots of John Innes No. 1 potting compost, or a peat-based equivalent.

Half- or semi-ripe cuttings are rooted in exactly the same way, but they are slightly longer – 8–10 cm (3–4 in) – and taken later in the summer when the stems are firmer to the touch. This type of cutting

Patient gardeners who don't rush their plants will be well rewarded by the leaf colouring of *Actinidia kolomikta*, provided it likes the spot chosen for it.

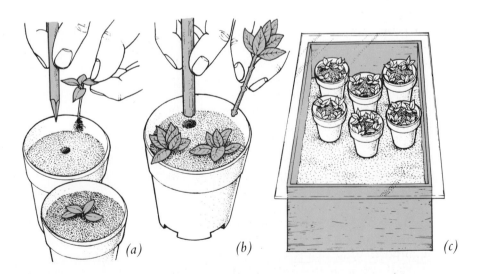

Fig. 15 (a) Transplanting seedlings into individual pots; (b) prepared softwood cuttings being dibbed into pots; (c) a simple propagating frame

may be taken with a 'heel'; that is, torn from the main stem with a small piece of hard wood. The 'tail' of this heel is trimmed before the cuttings are dipped in rooting powder and dibbed into pots (Fig. 16a).

Clematis cuttings are prepared rather differently. Lengths of semi-ripe stem are cut into sections, the top cut on each cutting being made above a pair of leaves, and the bottom cut between two leaf joints. This is known as an internodal cutting (Fig. 16b).

Hardwood cuttings are taken in autumn when the wood is fully hardened. They are often naked of foliage and they are prepared as follows: remove lengths of strong one-year-old stem from the plants to be propagated, cutting them above a leaf joint at the top and below a leaf joint at the base, to make them 25 cm (10 in) long. Remove all but

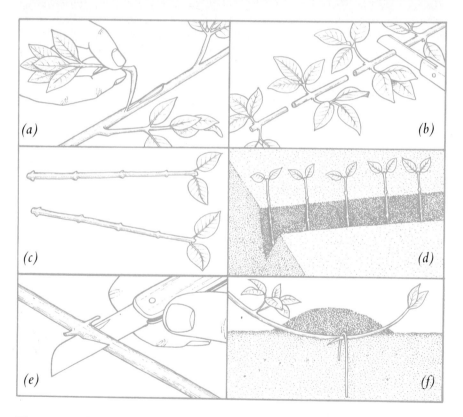

Fig. 16 (a) Semi-ripe cutting with 'heel' being removed from a shrub; (b) clematis (internodal) cutting; (c) prepared hardwood cuttings; (d) hardwood cuttings being inserted into V-shaped trench; (e) – (f) ground-layering a suitable stem

the topmost leaves. Dip the stem bases in rooting powder and insert the cuttings to two-thirds their depth outdoors in a 'V'-shaped trench lined with a little sand to ensure good drainage. Replace and firm the soil. The cuttings should grow away through the following summer and can be transplanted to their permanent sites in winter (Fig. 16c – d).

LAYERING

Pendent shoots of a variety of climbers and wall plants can be made to root when they come into contact with the ground. The convenient shoot, which should be woody and not soft, is cut with a knife so that a 'tongue' is made where the stem touches the ground (preferably 30 – 45 cm, 12 – 18 in, from the shoot tip). The cut surface is then dusted with rooting powder and the stem pegged down with a piece of wire. A small mound of soil is then placed over the stem (Fig. 16e – f). When the shoot has rooted into the soil it can be severed from its parent and transplanted to its permanent site.

DIVISION

Clump-forming plants are easily increased by division. Lift their roots in the dormant season between late autumn and early spring, and tease these apart to make smaller clumps which can be replanted immediately in their new situations.

Some plants throw up suckers (shoots arising directly from the roots) and these can be removed with a portion of the root system and transplanted in the same way.

CHAPTER 8

PESTS, DISEASES AND DISORDERS

The following table shows the pests, diseases and disorders most likely to prove troublesome in gardens. It is unlikely that you will encounter them all, particularly if you grow your plants well and pay attention to feeding, mulching, watering and pruning. Prompt action can prevent pest and disease outbreaks from getting out of hand, but in all cases avoid spraying when bees are about and flowers are open – they will both suffer. Follow the manufacturer's instructions to the letter and store all chemicals in a safe place out of the reach of children and pets.

Pest, disease or disorder	Plants most frequently affected	Symptoms	Control
Aphids (greenfly)	Wide range	Green, black or pink flies found sucking sap at shoot tips	Spray with pirimicarb, derris or malathion
Blackspot	Roses	Black spots on leaves	Spray with benomyl. Remove fallen leaves in winter.
Brown scale	Ceanothus, pyracantha, cotoneaster, roses	Small brown scales found on stems and leaves	Spray with malathion
Bud drop	Camellia	Flower buds fall before opening	Keep a thick mulch on ground. Water well in dry weather.
Capsid bug	Roses, fuchsia, hydrangea	Shoots distorted and pin-prick holes in leaves	Spray with HCH
Caterpillars	Wide range	Leaves and young stems eaten away	Spray with HCH or derris
Chlorosis	Hydrangea, camellia	Leaves turn yellow between veins	Water with diluted iron sequestrene
Dieback	Roses	Stems turn brown at cut surfaces and disease spreads backwards	Prune in early spring – not earlier. Cut out infected wood.
Earwigs	Clematis and annuals	Leaves and young stems eaten	Trap in flower pots filled with straw and upturned on bamboo canes

Pest, disease or disorder	Plants most frequently affected	Symptoms	Control
Fireblight	Pyracantha, cotoneaster, chaenomeles	Leaves and stems wilt and turn brown. Leaves do not fall	Dig up and burn
Honey fungus	Wide range	Plant wilts and dies. Black 'bootlaces' will be found among roots when dug up. Honey-coloured toadstools may appear	Remove all roots of infected plants. Sterilize area with Bray's Emulsion
Leaf-rolling sawfly	Roses	Leaves roll inwards to form scrolls	Spray with HCH at 2-week intervals from mid-spring
Powdery mildew	Roses, clematis, hydrangeas	White powdery deposit on leaves and stems	Spray with benomyl
Red spider mite	Roses	Minute reddish-brown mites found on undersides of leaves. Leaves become bleached	Spray with malathion or derris
Scorch	Wide range	Leaves turn brown at edges and become dry and crisp	Replant in more sheltered spot. Water well in dry periods
Slugs	Wide range, especially annuals	Leaves and young stems eaten. Slimy trails left behind	Lay poisoned baits under tiles. Sink yoghurt cartons containing beer into the ground as traps
Virus disease	Limited range	Leaves become mottled, wrinkled and distorted. Plant lacks vigour	Dig up and burn
Wilt	Clematis	Shoots wilt and die very suddenly	Cut out all affected stems. Water soil with benomyl
Woolly aphid	Pyracantha, cotoneaster	Woolly clusters containing aphids found on stems which become swollen	Spray with malathion

INDEX